CONFESSIONS OF A BORN-AGAIN CATHOLIC

A Scriptural Look at Catholic Christianity

By Daniel F. Wiegand

NIHIL OBSTAT: Rev. Msgr. John P. Zenz
Censor Deputatus

IMPRIMATUR: Adam Cardinal Maida
Archbishop of Detroit

First published by Dog Ear Publishing
4010 W. 86th Street, Ste H
Indianapolis, IN 46268
www.dogearpublishing.net

ISBN: 978-160844-747-3

This book is printed on acid-free paper.

Printed in the United States of America

FOREWORD BY
DR. FRANS M.J. BRANDT, EdD, LPC, ABMP

I have been blessed, enlightened, and inspired by Daniel Wiegand's book, *Confessions of a Born-Again Catholic*. This book delivers a whole lot more than one might assume from its title. Wiegand is an intelligent and highly persuasive author who presents an incredibly clear and convincing explanation of the importance of the teachings, practices, and traditions of the Catholic Church.

I immensely enjoyed reading this book because of the truly Christian spirit in which it has been written and the honest and dispassionate assessment of what the author believed went right and wrong during the Reformation. Both Catholic and non-Catholic Christians—as well as anyone who has even the slightest interest in the Bible, religion, spirituality, or church history—will be greatly blessed by reading this book.

Wiegand has written the kind of book, perhaps even *the* book, that may play a major role in bringing about greater unity to the body of Christ. This is also a very timely book. As we look at the fragmentation within many denominational churches, the deletion of entire parts of God's Word—or utter silence about many flagrant violations of it—then it becomes self-evident that, perhaps at no time since the formation of the early church has there been a greater need for a church that unequivocally upholds the Word of God.

Christians of every denomination and persuasion will do well to take a close look at this outstanding and much-needed book. If nothing else, *Confessions of a Born-Again Catholic* will bring many a reader into a closer, happier, and more fulfilling relationship with our Creator. Our wonderful God of light, life and love.

Frans M.J. Brandt
Consultant Psychotherapist
Author of *The Power of Winning Thinking, Victory over Depression, The Consistent Overcomer*, and other books

Dedication

To Cindy, who helped lead me to the Lord. To Father Jim Mayworm, who nurtured my newfound faith. To my parents, who planted the seeds of faith in my life. To my darling wife, Kathy, who has shown me so much about Christian living. To my three wonderful children, who have grown to adulthood in the grace and knowledge of the Lord. To my awesome grandchildren, who are precious gifts from God. To Dr. Frans M.J. Brandt for his enthusiastic support and encouraging words. To my good friend Al Luther for his editorial insights. Most of all, to the Lord Jesus Christ and the Holy Spirit, without whose prompting and guidance this book would not have been possible.

DISCLAIMER

This book is designed to provide information and express the author's opinions, supported by sacred Scripture, in regard to the subject matter covered. It is sold with the understanding that the author and publisher are not speaking in an official capacity on behalf of the Roman Catholic Church. It is not the purpose of this book to reprint all of the information available on the subject matter but to complement, amplify, and supplement other texts. You are urged to read other available material to learn as much as possible about the subject matter. For more information, see the references included in the Bibliography as well as the *Catechism of the Catholic Church.*

Every effort has been made to make this book as accurate as possible; however, there may be mistakes, both typographical and content related. This book should therefore be used only as a general reference and personal reflection, and not as the ultimate guide on the subject matter.

The purpose of this book is to educate, explain, and inform. The author and publisher shall have no liability or responsibility to those with contrary viewpoints, or for any loss or damage caused, or alleged to be caused, directly or indirectly, by the contents of this book.

There is a good possibility that you will find at least something in this book that you do not agree with 100%. That's OK. As Philippians 4:8 says, "Finally, brethren, whatever is true, whatever is honorable, whatever is just, whatever is pure, whatever is lovely, whatever is gracious, if there is any excellence, if there is anything worthy of praise, think about these things."

Contents

"If you continue in my word, you are truly my disciples, and you will know the truth, and the truth will make you free." (John 8:31-32)

Preface

Why did I write this book? I wrote it, first of all, because I felt led by the Lord to write it. "Compelled" is perhaps more accurate a term. Jeremiah 20:9 describes the feeling well: "There is in my heart as it were a burning fire shut up in my bones, and I am weary with holding it in, and I cannot."

I wrote this book because there is a lot of confusion and misunderstanding between Catholics and Protestants. There are those who say the Catholic Church is not scriptural. There are even those who say that it is a cult. I would like to address and hopefully resolve some of this confusion by setting forth scriptural authority for Catholic traditions and doctrines. Although there have been some improvements in Catholic-Protestant relations in the years between writing this book and getting it published, there is still considerable confusion and misunderstanding between the two.

I wrote this book because there is an appalling lack of unity in the Body of Christ. This lack of unity severely weakens the Body of Christ and its testimony to the world. Christians desperately need to understand and respect each other and work together for the salvation of the world. It is my prayer that this book will promote such unity.

I wrote this book because after becoming a born-again Christian, I became a born-again Catholic. I rediscovered a Catholic Church that is deeply spiritual, rich in symbolism and tradition, and definitely scriptural.

In Matthew 7:7, Jesus encourages us to ask, to seek, and to knock. The Catholic Church of today is a church that is asking, seeking, and knocking. It is a church that is learning, growing, and changing. This doesn't mean it is ready to jump on every new theological bandwagon that comes along. The Church moves slowly and cautiously, sort of like the turtle racing the hare. But the point is, it does move and it does change. We are a pilgrim church, plodding along slowly and steadily toward that glorious finish line, the Kingdom of God. We are a church that is growing deeper and deeper into the Word of God. The deeper we go, the more challenging our church becomes. This is as it should be, because the message Jesus preached was a total, life-changing commitment, a revolution within ourselves. No longer can we follow certain "thou shalt nots" and consider ourselves saved.

As I wrote this book, I prayed that the Holy Spirit would guide me and that His purpose would be accomplished. I now pray that each person who is meant to read this book will read it and be edified by it. And for those who may have been critical of the Catholic Church in the past or who have been influenced by such criticism, I urge you to open your minds and hearts and consider the words of 2 Corinthians 10:7: "Look at what is before your eyes. If anyone is confident that he is Christ's, let him remind himself that as he is Christ's, so are we."

"Faith is the substance of things hoped for, the evidence of things that are not seen." (Hebrews 11:1)

CHAPTER I

In the Beginning—Again

The Author's Testimony

I was born into a good Catholic family in 1946 and raised in the pre-Vatican II Church. We went to Mass every Sunday, abstained from meat on Friday, and said our prayers before and after meals and at night. I went to catechism every week, made my first communion, and was confirmed. I knew God was important but can't really say I had a close personal relationship with Him. When I prayed, I said the standard Catholic prayers. I knew nothing about the Bible.

My secular education went on through high school, college, and law school, but my spiritual education stopped at about the eighth-grade level. The Baltimore Catechism had given me all the answers, but it hadn't always explained how the answers were arrived at. It was a little like having a math book with the answers to all the problems. Things are easier for a while, but eventually, you have to learn to solve the problems for yourself. Paul says in 1 Corinthians 13:11, "When I was a child, I spoke like a child, I thought like a child, I reasoned like a child; when I became a man, I gave up childish ways." My problem was that in spiritual matters, I hadn't given up childish ways. I still thought like a child, spoke like a child, and reasoned like a child.

1 Peter 3:15 says we should always be prepared to make a defense to anyone who calls us to account for the hope that is in us. We should know what we believe and why. We should be able to defend our beliefs. I couldn't. When I went to college it was like a lamb going to the slaughter. I was exposed to Plato, Socrates, Aristotle, Nietzsche, Voltaire, Zen Buddhism, transcendental meditation, and many other philosophies and ideas. I continued going to the Catholic Church because that was what I grew up with, but I came out of college feeling that the Church didn't really make much difference.

In Colossians 2:8, Paul says, "See to it that no one makes a prey of you by philosophy and empty deceit, according to human tradition, according to the elemental spirits of the universe, and not according to

Christ." This would be good advice for any young person going away to college. I heard a lot of philosophy and human tradition in my classes, but not much Christianity. By the time I graduated I had a sort of "I'm OK, you're OK" philosophy. Whatever I believe is OK as long as it doesn't hurt you, and whatever you believe is OK as long as it doesn't hurt me. Everything is relative. There is no absolute truth. If we live "good lives," we will probably make it to heaven.

The problem is, who defines a "good life?" Man is infinitely capable of rationalizing anything he wants to do. Proverbs 14:12 says, "There is a way which seems right to a man, but its end is the way to death." God is the only one who can define truth and goodness. His word says that His thoughts are not our thoughts and His ways are not our ways (Isaiah 55:8,9). We have all sinned and fallen short of the glory of God (Romans 3:23). We have all gone astray and turned to our own way (Isaiah 53:6). No one is righteous (Romans 3:10). If we say we have no sin, we are only deceiving ourselves (1 John 1:8). Thus, by God's definition, none of us is good enough to deserve eternal life.

From 1969, when I graduated from college, until January 29, 1976, I would describe my spiritual state as "drifting." I believed in God, of course, but that is no great intellectual achievement. Only a fool would say there is no God (Psalms 14:1; 53:1). The wonders of nature declare His existence (Psalms 19:1-6). Everything from the vastness of the universe to the intricate colorings of a tiny insect, the incredible complexity of the human body, a human cell, the atom, the variety of plant and animal life, snowflakes and fingerprints—each one different—all the individual drops of water it took to fill all the rivers and oceans of the world, all the individual grains of sand to create all the beaches and deserts proclaim the existence of God. We not only have a Creator, but a Creator with supernatural artistic power. He paints the sky with glorious sunsets, sunrises, clouds, and rainbows. As Job chapter 38 demonstrates so beautifully, only God can answer the great questions of the universe.

I had no problem believing there was a God out there somewhere, but I wasn't convinced that he was concerned about the intricate details of my life and what I did or didn't do. The idea that for me to get to heaven, this all-powerful Creator of the universe had to become a man, be born in an animal manger, and eventually suffer humiliating torture and death on a cross didn't really make sense to my "college-enlightened mind." But then this isn't surprising. The Bible tells us that the idea of God becoming man and being crucified for our salvation is a "stumbling block to Jews and folly to Gentiles" (1 Corinthians 1:23). "The word of the cross is folly to those who are perishing" (1 Corinthians 1:18), yet "God chose what is foolish in the world to shame the wise" (1 Corinthians 1:27), "For the foolishness of God is wiser than men, and the weakness of God is stronger than men" (1 Corinthians 1:25).

In addition to graduating from college in 1969, I got married and started law school. My wife, Kathy, was the greatest blessing in my life. We had (and have) a terrific marriage. Our first child, Judy, was born in 1973. I had everything going for me; but like the young man in Mark 10:21, I still lacked one thing, the most important thing: a personal relationship with Jesus Christ. We continued going to church every Sunday, but for me it was just a religious habit.

About that time,(1973), I had an eighteen-year-old relative who became a so called "Jesus freak." One day I asked her, "What's all this Jesus stuff you're into?" She responded with a most challenging question: "Dan, you know Jesus is real, don't you?" It was essentially that same soul-piercing question Jesus asked his disciples in Matthew 16:15: "But who do you say that I am?"

The question forced me to confront my agnosticism about Jesus. Deep inside, I had to admit that I wasn't sure I believed in Jesus anymore. I answered, halfheartedly, "Well, yeah, I know He's real, but you really can't prove it, can you?"

My relative confidently replied that there were so many proofs of Jesus, she would hardly know where to begin. She introduced me to a few of the startling prophecies about Jesus in the Old Testament such as Psalm 22 and Isaiah 53. I decided I would study the Bible (for the first time in my life) and give God a chance. I didn't want to reject the truth, but I also didn't want to go through the motions of pretending to believe. Like Thomas, my legalistic mind wanted proof. I soon found out that God was equal to the challenge.

Chapter 24 of Luke's Gospel illustrates that Jesus used the technique of citing Old Testament prophecies to prove who He was. In the account of Jesus and his disciples walking on the road to Emmaus after his resurrection, Luke 24:27 says, "And beginning with Moses and all the prophets, he interpreted to them in all the Scriptures the things concerning himself." This is exactly what happened to me as I began to study the Bible. I cannot explain why it was necessary for God to become man and die for our sins, but I began to see how this had been specifically and repeatedly prophesied throughout the Old Testament.

There are two distinct lines of prophecy throughout the Old Testament. One relates to the end times, when the Messiah will come to save the world from destruction and establish his kingdom on earth. The other line, which is a little more subtle, relates to the first coming of Christ, when he would suffer and die for our sins. In the very beginning, when God created man, He said, "Let us make man in our image, after our likeness . . ." (Genesis 1:26). He didn't say, "Let me make man in *my* image." Thus, right from the outset we have the inference that God is more than one person.

As John puts it so beautifully in his Gospel, chapter one, verses 1 through 3: "In the beginning was the Word, and the Word was with God, and the Word was God. He was in the beginning with God; all things were made through him, and without him was not anything made that was made." Colossians 1:16 says that "in Him all things were created." In other words, Jesus was involved in creation itself. Interestingly, this is one of the statements contained in the Catholic Creed that we say at Mass every Sunday: "We believe in one Lord, Jesus Christ, the only son of God, eternally begotten of the Father, God from God, Light from Light, true God from true God, begotten, not made, one in being with the Father. *Through him all things were made.*"

There are many "types" or symbols of Jesus in the Old Testament. The blood sacrifice of the Passover Lamb in Exodus 12 is perhaps the most obvious. It is the blood of the Lamb (Jesus) that saves us. Just as Moses threw the blood on the people in Exodus 24:8, we must be covered by the blood of the Lamb to enter into this salvation covenant. Exodus 12:5 says that the lamb must be without blemish. Only Jesus is without the blemish of sin. He is referred to as "the Lamb of God" in New Testament Scriptures such as John 1:29 and 1 Corinthians 5:7. In Psalm 23 and Isaiah 40:11, the Lord is referred to as our shepherd. In John 10:11, Jesus reveals that He is this shepherd. He is both our shepherd and our lamb. He is everything we need—the Alpha and the Omega.

One of the most beautiful types or symbols of the sacrifice of Jesus for our sins is the story of Abraham and Isaac in Genesis 22. Isaac was Abraham's only son, just as Jesus is God's only son. Isaac's birth was miraculous, just as Jesus' birth was miraculous. Abraham was 99 years old, and Sarah was well beyond child bearing age when she conceived. In verse 2, God says to Abraham, "Take your son, your only son Isaac, whom you love, and go to the land of Moriah, and offer him there as a burnt offering upon one of the mountains of which I shall tell you." In verse 6, Isaac is made to carry the wood for his sacrifice. In verse 8, as they approach the place of the sacrifice, Abraham says, "God will provide *himself* the lamb for a burnt offering, my son." This verse seems to have a double meaning. God did intervene and provide a ram for Abraham to sacrifice (verse 13), thus stopping Abraham from having to sacrifice his son. I believe the point of this beautiful story, however, was to show us that God would provide "Himself" (His own Son) as the sacrificial lamb for our salvation.

The deeper I went into my Bible study, the more I found that everything about Jesus was symbolized and prophesied in detail hundreds and even thousands of years before His birth. Finally, I reached the inescapable conclusion that Jesus really was the Messiah. He was and is God the Son. Meanwhile, my Bible-tutor relative kept urging me to pray for salvation. She showed me where the Bible said that to enter the Kingdom of God, we must be "born anew" (John 3:3); we must admit that we are sinners (Romans 3:23, 1 John 1:8); we must repent of our sins (Mark 1:15, Luke 13:3); we must believe in Jesus (Mark 16:16, John 3:18); we must become as children, childlike in our faith and dependence upon God (Matthew 18:3); we must acknowledge Jesus as our Lord and Savior (Matthew 10:32, Romans 10:9-10).

At first I was reluctant. I found lots of excuses: I wasn't ready yet, I hadn't studied it enough. I realize now that Satan did not want me to pray that prayer for salvation. But once you come to the point where you believe the Bible is the true, inspired Word of God and that Jesus is the Messiah, God the Son, you simply cannot ignore it. I was finally convinced that this was what I must do. For the first time I can remember, I prayed a spontaneous prayer directly to God that went something like this:

> *Lord God, I come to You a sinner, knowing I have doubted You and rejected You in many ways in my life. But now I believe in You, Jesus. I believe that You died for all my sins and that You offer me the free gift of salvation. Lord Jesus, I*

repent now and promise to try and live according to Your will as revealed in the Bible. I ask for forgiveness in Your name Jesus, and I ask You to come into my heart right now, to save me, to give me the gift of the Holy Spirit and the gift of eternal life. I thank You Lord. Amen.

I can't explain it, but right then and there, in my living room on January 29, 1976, I was "born anew." You may choose to call it being born from above, a spiritual awakening, a conversion experience, being born of the Spirit, a spiritual birth, or some other term. No matter what semantics you use, it was the major spiritual turning point in my life. I had been heading away from the Kingdom of God; now I was heading toward it. I knew my sins had been forgiven. I had been redeemed. I realized that Jesus was my Savior. I was a new creation, a different person (2 Corinthians 5:17). I had peace with God (Romans 5:1). I knew I had eternal life (1 John 5:13). I had returned to the shepherd and guardian of my soul (1 Peter 2:25). The blood of Jesus had cleansed me from all sin (1 John 1:7). I was a child of God (John 1:12-13).

Witnessing

One of the first signs of being born again is the desire to tell everyone about it and convince them that they need the same thing. Like the woman at the well in John 4:28–29, I couldn't wait to share the good news with my family, my friends, and anyone else who would listen. The problem was, I had been led to believe that everyone had to come to the Lord the same way I did. I had a great sense of urgency because I thought people wouldn't go to heaven unless they went through the same steps I had. I had no hesitancy in going up to the people who had been Catholic all their lives and telling them that they needed to be born again. What I didn't realize is that many of them already were.

Eventually, I came to understand that being born again isn't always a sudden change like it was with me. It isn't always an intellectual decision like it was with me. I know that Paul had a dramatic conversion (Acts 9:3-9, 17-19; 22:6-16). He called himself the "foremost of sinners" (1 Timothy 1:15). This is not just false humility on his part. Paul vehemently persecuted those of the Christian faith (Acts 9:1-3, 13; 22:4, 19-20); so when he was converted, he really received the message of grace. If God could forgive him, He could forgive anyone! But what about the other apostles? I don't think they had such sudden, dramatic conversions. I think their conversions were more gradual. Certainly, they came to the knowledge of who Jesus was and they were born again, but it wasn't a sudden, immediate thing. In fact, they seem to have struggled somewhat with the question of exactly who Jesus was until after the resurrection.

The issue is not how we get to the point of knowing Jesus as our Lord and Savior; only that we get there. We come to the Lord in many different ways. Some people can't say when they actually accepted Jesus, but they believe in Him and know He is their Lord and Savior. Some may come by receiving the sacrament of reconciliation after being away from the Church for a while. Some may come to the Lord as the result of a crisis in their lives. Some may come through seeing a loved one healed in answer to prayer. The Bible says, "No one can say 'Jesus is Lord' except by the Holy Spirit" (1 Corinthians 12:3); "Whoever confesses that Jesus is the Son of God, God abides in him, and he in God" (1 John 4:15). "God is love, and he who abides in love abides in God, and God abides in him" (1 John 4:16). So if a person can say Jesus is Lord and really mean it, that person has received the Holy Spirit; and if a person "abides in love," God abides in that person, and he or she has had a spiritual birth.

How, then, should we go about sharing the good news and evangelizing? In my early attempts at witnessing I tried the hard-sell approach. I tried the rehearsed speech. For the most part these things didn't work. I think the best instruction the Bible gives on witnessing is in Mark 5:19, where Jesus tells a man who had been delivered from demonic possession, "Go home to your friends, and tell them how much the Lord has done for you, and how he has had mercy on you." Mark 5:20 says, "And he went away and began to proclaim in the Decapolis how much Jesus had done for him; and all men marveled." I believe this is the most effective way to witness. We need to tell people what the Lord has done for us and how He has had mercy on us. We need to share our testimony with them. We don't need to tell them what is wrong with them and what they need. They will figure that out on their own.

In John 13:35, Jesus tells us another way to witness. He says, "By this all men will know that you are my disciples, if you have love for one another." We shouldn't have to tell people we're Christians. They should realize that simply by the love we have for one another.

Another way to witness is through our good works. In Matthew 5:16, Jesus says, "Let your light so shine before men, that they may see your good works and give glory to your Father who is in heaven." In other words, actions do speak louder than words. It is said that St. Francis once told his monks, "Go out and preach the gospel. If necessary, use words." We do have an obligation to acknowledge Jesus before men, to speak about Him and to teach the Word (Deuteronomy 6:6-7; Matthew 10:32; Luke 9:26; Colossians 3:16), but talking the talk is not going to do any good unless we also walk the walk. Why did the world listen so intently to the words of Mother Teresa? It wasn't that her words were so powerful or dynamic. They listened because she preached the Gospel by her total life, not just her words.

Christian Critics

As a newly reborn Christian, I was eager to find other Christians to fellowship and share the Word with; but most of the people I found who talked about Jesus and the Bible seemed to have a decidedly anti-Catholic viewpoint. They told me the Catholic Church wasn't scriptural. They couldn't understand how I could be born again and still be Catholic. They thought Catholics were "unsaved." They criticized Catholic traditions and doctrines. They said the Catholic Bible had some "extra books" that weren't divinely inspired. Some went so far as to say the Catholic Church was a cult and the pope could even be the Antichrist. Needless to say, I was shocked and confused by these assertions. These people seemed sincere and appeared to know a lot more about the Bible than I did. I eventually discovered that these other Christians didn't know as much about the Bible as I (and they) thought they did.

In 1 Timothy 6:4, Paul warns about people who have "a morbid craving for controversy and for disputes about words." He says these things produce "envy, dissension, slander and base suspicions." I seemed to encounter a lot of these people in my early born-again days. They said they were Christians, but they were more concerned with the specks in their neighbors' eyes than the logs in their own eyes (Matthew 7:3). I remember being invited to a prayer meeting on one occasion. I was looking forward to a time of prayer and fellowship with a group of Bible-believing Christians. Instead, the prayer meeting turned out to be a cross-examination of my Catholic beliefs. I began to think that perhaps all these people were right. Perhaps I was in the wrong church.

I had to admit that the Catholic Church I was attending at the time was very conservative and very traditional. It didn't seem to emphasize the Bible very much. There was no formal Bible study program and no charismatic (explained in Chapter IX) prayer group. I naturally assumed that all other Catholic churches would be exactly the same. I wanted a church that really preached the Word of God and had all the zeal and enthusiasm of the early Christian church. I thought I would have to change denominations to find that. Thus, I began my search for the "perfect church."

As I started going to different Protestant churches, I found some that specialized in criticizing other denominations. Other churches frankly seemed a bit phony to me. During the sermon, people would occasionally shout out "Amen," but it seemed almost forced rather than sincere and spontaneous. Some churches spoke against the gifts of the Holy Spirit and even said the charismatic movement was of the devil. Other churches went to the opposite extreme; they were too charismatic for me. They put me in a room with a bunch of people who were praying in tongues in a very loud and exuberant manner; then they tried to get me to do the same thing. I couldn't. I felt out of place and very uncomfortable. In some churches I found the music and worship to be less inspiring than in the Catholic church I had been attending. They might have a good sermon, but that was about it. I felt that something was lacking.

Then one day I heard about St. Lucy's, a Catholic Church in St. Clair Shores, Michigan, not more than a mile from my house. It had a "Spirit-filled" priest who actually had a Bible study every Wednesday night. I decided to go the next Wednesday night and check it out. What a shock! This priest came bounding into the room with a big Bible, a big smile, and an armful of notes. He was "aglow with the Spirit" (Romans 12:11). He greeted people warmly, shaking hands and even hugging and kissing some of them. He started with a prayer, but it wasn't a traditional Catholic prayer. It was spontaneous. Other people from the group joined in and added their prayers and intentions. I could really sense the presence of God in that room. This priest, Father

Jim Mayworm, and these people obviously had a deep faith in Jesus and a love of His Word!

I came home and told my wife that I'd found the right church. I think she was relieved that I wasn't going to ask her to switch denominations. The sermons were great! The music was terrific and imaginative! They had a charismatic prayer group. They even had liturgical dance and drama. I felt very much at home at St. Lucy's, and I thank God for leading me there. It was tough when Father Jim was transferred to another parish, but the Spirit of the Lord remained with our community. Eventually we were blessed with another wonderful Spirit-filled and gifted pastor, Rev. Bohdan Kosicki. I felt very much at home at St. Lucy's, and my family remained there for almost 20 years until a job change moved us to Frankenmuth, Michigan. Even though I've been here for over 15 years, I still miss St. Lucy's and my many dear friends and faith partners there. I look forward to renewing these friendships in heaven some day. But I can also see that God has used me in my new location.

Some people change churches because they don't like the pastor, or because their church doesn't seem Spirit filled enough, or it's too conservative, or because they just don't feel comfortable there. I think it's important to pray about it and let God put us where He wants us. After moving to Frankenmuth, I heard about a charismatic Catholic church in Montrose, Michigan (not far from Frankenmuth). I prayed and asked God if I should go there. The response was "Why do they need another charismatic in Montrose?" So I'll stay where I'm at unless and until I'm sure that God is leading me elsewhere. Don't get me wrong; the church I attend right now is a good one. It's not exactly like St. Lucy's, but we do have a very good pastor and the church is growing in the Lord. More importantly, God has made it clear to me that this is the church where He wants me at this point in my life.

It's important to note that although this book has received the Imprimatur and Nihil Obstat (the Catholic Church's seal of approval), I don't claim to be an official spokesman for the Catholic Church. I'm not an ordained priest. But in my spiritual growth and development since January 29, 1976, I have gained a new appreciation for the Catholic Church. It is my prayer that this book will help others to gain that same appreciation. I realize that the Catholic Church is not composed of perfect people. I am painfully aware of the recent scandals involving some of its clergy. But you don't condemn an entire profession such as accounting, law, medicine, or politics because of the wrongful acts of a few of its members. Likewise, we shouldn't condemn the Catholic clergy or the Catholic Church, with a history going back more than 2000 years, for the recently revealed indiscretions of a small minority of its clergy. And to say that the Catholic Church is not scriptural or that it is a cult is simply untrue, unfounded, and unfair.

Homework

If you have not done so already, I would encourage you to look up the Scripture verses cited in the preceding pages. As you continue to read this book, I would also suggest that you keep your Bible at your side so you can look up the verses as you go. It may take more time, but you will find it to be an enriching and edifying exercise.

If you have never prayed to accept and receive Jesus as your Lord and Savior, I would encourage you to pray the prayer set forth on pages **5** and **6**. If you pray this prayer sincerely from the bottom of your heart, you too can experience the peace and joy of being a new creation in Christ Jesus.

CHAPTER II

Salvation

Saying It Isn't Enough

If there are any two questions that emphasize the division between Protestantism and Catholicism they are: "Are you saved?" and "Is salvation by faith or by works?" Ask these questions of an evangelical Protestant and you will probably receive direct, definite, and absolute answers: "Yes, I'm saved," and "Salvation is strictly by faith. Works have nothing to do with it." Ask the average Catholic these same questions and the answers probably won't be so simple, direct, and absolute.

If the evangelical Christians are correct, then sincere Catholics are just as "saved" as they are. Catholics believe that Jesus is God the Son; that He was born of the Virgin Mary and became man; that for our salvation He suffered and died on the cross; that He rose from the dead and ascended into heaven; that He will come again to judge the living and the dead; and that without Jesus' sacrifice on Calvary none of us would get to heaven. We profess all of that every Sunday in our Creed. But if salvation means more than simply believing, if it means more than a mere profession of faith, if it means living out our Christian commitment for our entire life, then evangelical Christians are no more "saved" than Catholics.

I certainly do not mean to diminish the importance of being "born anew." As stated in Chapter I of this book, my born-again experience was the major spiritual turning point of my life. But eventually, I came to realize that being born again is only the beginning. Just as being married means more than going through a wedding ceremony, being saved means more than being born again. Being saved means living out the Christian commitment we make when we are born again. Like marriage, it means for better and for worse, for richer and for poorer, in good times and bad, in sickness and in health, until we die. We can't say that once we've been born again we've got it made, no matter what we do.

Does that mean we earn salvation by good works? No. Jesus is "the way, the truth, and the life," and no one comes to the Father but by

Him (John 14:6). Without His death on the cross, none of us would be saved. He is the door to salvation (John 10:9). There is salvation in no one else, and there is no other name given under heaven by which we must be saved (Acts 4:12). We need to believe in Jesus to receive eternal life (Mark 16:16; John 3:15-18; 6:40; 11:25-26). Acts 10:43 tells us that those who believe in Jesus receive forgiveness for their sins through His name. Catholics refer to this as "sanctifying grace." The issue isn't really whether or not we are saved by faith. We are saved by grace through faith. The question is, what is *faith* in the biblical sense? The Catholic position is that faith and works are so inextricably linked that you can't have one without the other.

Believing in Jesus means following Him and trying to do what He says. If we don't do that, we don't really have biblical faith. It isn't enough to say we believe or even to believe intellectually. We must believe in our hearts. Faith, in the scriptural sense, is manifested by action. It means making a commitment, a lifelong commitment, to try to live according to God's will as set forth in the Bible. Yes, when we fail to live up to that commitment, He forgives us. 1 John 2:1-2 tells us,

> My little children, I am writing this to you so that you may not sin; but if anyone does sin, we have an advocate with the Father, Jesus Christ the righteous; and he is the expiation for our sins, and not for ours only but also for the sins of the whole world.

But we must truly repent and truly believe. Faith is not a surface thing or a mere intellectual thing.

I don't want to heap more criticism on television evangelists. God knows they get enough of that these days. Most of them are sincere, and they do a lot of good. I must say, however, that I am occasionally dismayed to hear a televangelist assure people of salvation by praying a simple prayer like: "God, I need you in my life. I want to go to heaven. I want the gift of eternal life. I want to be saved. I want to be born again. Come into my heart now, Jesus, and save me." Of course they want all these things, but where is the repentance? Where is the commitment? Where does the prayer say that this person really believes in Jesus and will sincerely try to live in accordance with God's Word from that point forward?

If we are going to lead a person in a salvation prayer, we should do it right. We should go through the elements; explain what is required; ask if he is ready to accept Jesus not only as his savior but as Lord of his life. Does he mean to sincerely repent and live as a Christian from this point forward? The Bible says that we must repent (Mark 1:15), and that if we do not repent, we will all perish (Luke 13:3-5). This message should be brought out loud and clear when leading a person in a "sinner's prayer." Then, if he is ready to make that lifetime commitment, we can lead him through a true salvation prayer which encompasses all the elements.

What does the Bible say about the relationship between faith and works with regard to salvation? We can't just say "I like what Paul says about salvation. I'll stick with that." The Bible says, "The sum of thy word is truth" (Psalm 119:160). We have to take the Bible as a whole. We have to consider not only what Paul says but also what James says, what John says, what Jesus Himself says. Paul didn't reveal all the truth. If all the truth was revealed by any one Bible author or in any one book of the Bible, we wouldn't need the rest of the Bible.

In John 3:36 Jesus clearly explains the need for both faith and obedience. He says, "He who believes in the Son has eternal life; he who does not obey the Son shall not see life, but the wrath of God rests upon him." Faith and obedience go hand in hand. If we march up to the front of a church or go forward at a crusade and pray a sinner's prayer but then go on living our lives exactly as before, in disobedience to the Lord, we aren't saved. It is as simple as that.

I think James 2:14-26 is probably the Bible's clearest answer to the question of faith versus works:

> What does it profit, my brethren, if a man says he has faith but has not works? Can his faith save him? If a brother or sister is ill-clad and in lack of daily food, and one of you says to them, "Go in peace, be warmed and filled," without giving them the things needed for the body, what does it profit? So faith by itself, if it has no works, is dead.
>
> But someone will say, "You have faith and I have works." Show me your faith apart from your works, and I by my works will show you my faith. You believe that God is one; you do well. Even the demons believe—and shudder. Do you

want to be shown you foolish fellow, that faith apart from works is barren? Was not Abraham our father justified by works, when he offered his son Isaac upon the altar? You see that faith was active along with his works, and faith was completed by works, and the Scripture was fulfilled which says, "Abraham believed God, and it was reckoned to him as righteousness"; and he was called the friend of God. You see that a man is justified by works and not by faith alone. And in the same way was not also Rahab the harlot justified by works when she received the messengers and sent them out another way? For as the body apart from the spirit is dead, so faith apart from works is dead.

It is almost as if James anticipated the argument that we are saved by faith alone and that works have nothing to do with it. If we have faith, our faith will be manifested by our works. This is basically the Catholic position on salvation, and I believe it is consistent with the Bible taken as a whole.

Salvation According to Paul

Certainly, one of the greatest saints in the Bible is Paul. He wrote more of the New Testament than anyone else. In the Catholic Church we have a reading from Paul's letters at almost every Mass. They are beautiful, edifying, and definitive on Christian doctrine. There is no question that Paul stressed salvation by grace through faith. I think there are two primary reasons for this emphasis. First, Paul had a dramatic, sudden conversion. He experienced the forgiveness of God in a very special way. Second, Paul was the apostle to the Gentiles. He had to overcome the idea that because the Gentiles didn't keep all the Jewish laws and rituals, they couldn't be saved. He therefore stressed the fact that we are not saved by religious works and rituals. We are saved (redeemed, justified) by Jesus' sacrifice on Calvary.

But I think Paul is misunderstood at times. Paul didn't preach a quick and easy salvation by praying a simple prayer and accepting Jesus intellectually. He preached a life-changing commitment. He preached a life of self-sacrifice and obedience. The conversion envisioned by Paul is dying to the flesh and living in the Spirit, making no provision for the flesh

(Romans 13:14). In Romans 6:2 Paul says, "How can we who died to sin still live in it?" We are to walk in newness of life (Romans 6:4). We must consider ourselves dead to sin and alive to God through Christ Jesus (Romans 6:11). We are to walk not according to the flesh but according to the Spirit (Romans 8:4). "For those who live according to the flesh set their minds on the things of the flesh, but those who live according to the Spirit set their minds on the things of the Spirit" (Romans 8:5).

Paul also emphasized the theme of reaping what we sow. In Romans 2:6-11 he says,

> For he will render to every man according to his works; to those who by patience in well-doing seek for glory and honor and immortality, he will give eternal life; but for those who are factious and do not obey the truth, but obey wickedness, there will be wrath and fury. There will be tribulation and distress for every human being who does evil, the Jew first and also the Greek, but glory and honor and peace for every-one who does good, the Jew first and also the Greek. For God shows no partiality.

In Galatians 6:7-8 he says,

> Do not be deceived; God is not mocked, for whatever a man sows, that he will also reap. For he who sows to his own flesh will from the flesh reap corruption; but he who sows to the Spirit will from the Spirit reap eternal life.

And in Galatians 5:19-21 Paul writes,

> Now the works of the flesh are plain: immorality, impurity, licentiousness, idolatry, sorcery, enmity, strife, jealousy, anger, selfishness, dissension, party-spirit, envy, drunkenness, carousing, and the like. I warn you as I warned you before, that those who do such things shall not inherit the kingdom of God.

To the church in Corinth, Paul pens these words:

Therefore let anyone who thinks that he stands take heed lest he fall. . . . For we must all appear before the judgment seat of Christ, so that each one may receive good or evil, according to what he has done in the body. (1 Corinthians 10:12; 2 Corinthians 5:10)

It is true that Paul did not emphasize religious works and rituals; but he did emphasize works of charity. In 1 Corinthians 15:58 he says, "Therefore, my beloved brethren, be steadfast, immovable, always abounding in the work of the Lord, knowing that in the Lord your labor is not in vain." In 1 Thessalonians 4:1 he says, "Finally, brethren, we beseech and exhort you in the Lord Jesus, that as you learned from us how you ought to live and to please God, just as you are doing, you do so more and more." Again, in Philippians 2:12 he writes, "Therefore, my beloved, as you have always obeyed, so now, not only as in my presence but much more in my absence, work out your own salvation with fear and trembling."

Salvation According to Jesus

Jesus didn't preach a quick and easy salvation either. If anything, He taught just the opposite. He said, "Enter by the narrow gate; for the gate is wide and the way is easy, that leads to destruction, and those who enter by it are many. For the gate is narrow and the way is hard, that leads to life, and those who find it are few" (Matthew 7:13-14). In Mark 10:24 Jesus told His disciples, "Children, how hard it is to enter the kingdom of God!" If you have a Bible with the words of Christ in red, I encourage you to go through the Gospels reading only Jesus' words, particularly noting what he said about salvation. You may find it surprising.

Consider the parable of the Good Samaritan (Luke 10:30-37). If anyone would be considered "saved," it would be the priest. Yet he did not fulfill the commandment of loving his neighbor. Next in line would be the Levite. The tribe of Levi was entrusted with the sacred responsibility of caring for the temple. They were considered to be very holy people. Yet the Levite also did not show love for his neighbor. If anyone was considered "unsaved" in Jesus' society, however, it would have been the people of Samaria. They were considered spiritual half-breeds and outcasts. Yet it was the Samaritan who fulfilled the commandment to love his neighbor. Jesus' message is clear: Our actions speak louder than our words or religious status.

Consider the parable of the father and the two sons in Matthew 21:28-32. One son *said* he would do as his father asked, but he didn't. The other son refused at first but then repented and *did* what his father asked. Again, actions speak louder than words. The parable of the talents in Luke 19:11-28 is also illustrative. Each of the servants received the same gift. Those who used their gifts to bear fruit were rewarded; but the one who did not bear fruit was punished. Perhaps the best example of Jesus' teaching on salvation is the parable of the sheep and goats in Matthew 25:31-46:

> When the Son of man comes in his glory, and all the angels with him, then he will sit on his glorious throne. Before him will be gathered all the nations, and he will separate them one from another as a shepherd separates the sheep from the goats, and he will place the sheep at his right hand, but the goats at the left.
>
> Then the King will say to those at his right hand, "Come, O blessed of my Father, inherit the kingdom prepared for you from the foundation of the world; for I was hungry and you gave me food, I was thirsty and you gave me drink, I was a stranger and you welcomed me, I was naked and you clothed me, I was sick and you visited me, I was in prison and you came to me."
>
> Then the righteous will answer him, "Lord, when did we see thee hungry and feed thee, or thirsty and give thee drink? And when did we see thee a stranger and welcome thee, or naked and clothe thee? And when did we see thee sick or in prison and visit thee?"
>
> And the King will answer them, "Truly, I say to you, as you did it to one of the least of these my brethren, you did it to

me." Then he will say to those at his left hand, "Depart from me, you cursed, into the eternal fire prepared for the devil and his angels; for I was hungry and you gave me no food, I was thirsty and you gave me no drink, I was a stranger and you did not welcome me, naked and you did not clothe me, sick and in prison and you did not visit me."

Then they will also answer, "Lord, when did we see thee hungry or thirsty or a stranger or naked or sick or in prison, and did not minister to thee?" Then he will answer them, "Truly, I say to you, as you did it not to one of the least of these, you did it not to me." And they will go away into eternal punishment, but the righteous into eternal life.

Is the emphasis on faith or works? If we don't feed the hungry, give drink to the thirsty, visit the sick and imprisoned, clothe the naked, welcome the stranger, etc., do you think we will be "saved" on Judgment Day when the Lord separates the sheep from the goats? Consider what Jesus says in Matthew 7:21-23:

Not every one who says to me, "Lord, Lord," shall enter the kingdom of heaven, but he who does the will of my Father who is in heaven. On that day many will say to me, "Lord, Lord, did we not prophesy in your name, and cast out demons in your name, and do many mighty works in your name?" And then I will declare to them, "I never knew you; depart from me, you evil doers."

It isn't enough just to hear the words of Jesus. It isn't enough even to "prophesy in his name, cast out demons in his name, and do mighty works in his name." We have to not only hear the Word of God but also do it (Luke 11:18). We need to keep Jesus' word and commandments (John 14:15, 21; John 14:33). We need to bear fruit (John 15:1-2). If we're going to follow Jesus, we need to count the cost and bear our crosses (Luke 14: 27-28). If we want to save our lives, we need to give them up (Mark 8:35; Matthew 10:39; Luke 9:24). If we want to be disciples of Jesus, we have to be willing to renounce everything else (Luke 14:33); we have to become servant of all (Mark 9:35); we have to persevere and endure to the end (Matthew 24:13; Luke 21:19). Then we'll be repaid for what we have done (Mark 16:27). These are challenging words. Jesus didn't preach an easy path to the kingdom. In fact, it isn't even possible to get there on our own. But the good news is that with God, all things are possible (Matthew 19:26). God enables us to live the Christian life, and if we fall short at times, He is there to forgive us.

Jesus clearly emphasized the importance of works. It isn't enough to just say you believe. It isn't enough to have an intellectual belief in Jesus. It isn't enough to be involved in church. It isn't enough to memorize Scripture verses. Yes, faith is essential; but it must be a faith that is manifested by works. Yes, we have to be born anew to see the kingdom of God (John 3:3); but being born anew is just the beginning. Just as physical birth is only the beginning of life, spiritual birth is only the beginning of our spiritual life. We must grow and develop to become spiritually mature. This means not only knowing the Word of God but making a sincere and continuing effort to live it.

Eternal Security?

Some denominations believe that once you're "saved," you can never be "lost." Once you've believed in Jesus and accepted him as your Lord and Savior; once you've gone forward and prayed the sinner's prayer; that clinches it forever. No matter what you do from that point on, you're saved. This belief is known as the eternal-security doctrine. It may be comforting, but is it scriptural? I don't think so. Consider the eternal-security doctrine in light of the following Scriptures:

For if, after they have escaped the defilements of the world through the knowledge of our Lord and Savior Jesus Christ, they are again entangled in them and overpowered, the last state has become worse for them than the first. For it would have been better for them never to have known the way of righteousness than after knowing it to turn back from the holy commandment delivered to them. (2 Peter 2:20-21)

Take care, brethren, lest there be in any of you an evil, unbelieving heart, leading you to fall away from the living God. (Hebrews 3:12)

For we share in Christ, if only we hold our first confidence firm to the end. (Hebrews 3:14)

If we endure, we shall also reign with him; if we deny him, he also will deny us. (2 Timothy 2:12)

Now I would remind you, brethren, in what terms I preached to you the gospel, which you received, in which you stand, by which you are saved, if you hold it fast—unless you believed in vain. (1 Corinthians 15:1-2)

And let us not grow weary in well doing, for in due season, we shall reap, if we do not lose heart. (Galatians 6:9)

If anyone does not provide for his relatives, and especially for his own family, he has disowned the faith and is worse than an unbeliever. (1 Timothy 5:8)

And you, who once were estranged and hostile in mind, doing evil deeds, he has now reconciled in his body of flesh by his death, in order to present you holy and blameless and irreproachable before him, provided that you continue in the faith, stable and steadfast, not shifting from the hope of the gospel which you heard, which has been preached to every creature under heaven, and of which I, Paul, became a minister. (Colossians 1:21-23)

Note then the kindness and the severity of God; severity toward those who have fallen, but God's kindness to you, provided you continue in his kindness; otherwise you too will be cut off. (Romans 11:22)

It is possible to fall away. It is possible to disown the faith. It is possible to turn back to sin. Philippians 3:12-14 shows that even Paul didn't assume he "had it made." He didn't consider that he had already obtained salvation or that he was already perfect, but he kept pressing on toward the mark. So must we.

The If's

We Christians love to quote and claim the promises of God. We like to claim the salvation verses as well. But there's a tiny word in many of these verses that we sometimes overlook. The word is "if." This one little word makes a whole promise conditional. It means that something is required on our part in order to receive what is promised.

In John 15:14, for example, Jesus says, "You are my friends *if* you do what I command you." (What if we don't do what he commands?) In John 13:17 Jesus says, "If you know these things, blessed are you *if* you do them." (It isn't enough to know the Word; we must do it.) In John 8:31-32 Jesus said to the Jews who had believed in him, "*If* you continue in my word, you are truly my disciples, and you will know the truth, and the truth will make you free." (Note, this was said to those who had believed in Him. The inference is that if they did not continue in His Word, they were not truly His disciples, they would not know the truth, and they would not be free.)

1 John 2:3 says, "And by this we may be sure that we know him, *if* we keep his commandments." (If we don't keep His commandments, we can't be sure we know Him.) And in John 15:10 Jesus says, "*If* you keep my commandments, you will abide in my love, just as I have kept my Father's commandments and abide in his love." (Can we really say we abide in God's love if we don't keep His commandments?) The promises of God are ours only if we meet the applicable conditions.

The Common Denominator

If there is any criteria to determine whether or not a person is saved, I believe that criteria is love. 1 John 4:7-8, 12, 20 say,

> Beloved, let us love one another; for love is of God, and he who loves is born of God and knows God. . . . He who does not love does not know God; for God is love. . . . No man has ever seen God; if we love one another, God abides in us and his love is perfected in us. . . . If anyone says, "I love God," and hates his brother, he is a liar; for he who does not love his brother whom he has seen, cannot love God whom he has not seen.

I believe love will be the common denominator in heaven. If we don't have love, we simply won't be there.

If you were to boil all of Jesus' commandments down to one word, that word would be "love." In John 13:34 Jesus says, "A new commandment I give to you, that you love one another; even as I have loved you, that you also love one another." (See also Mark 12:29-31; John 15:17.) Love is not optional; it is a commandment. And we aren't just to love our friends and relatives and the people who are easy to love; we are called to love our enemies and those we feel are unlovable (Luke 6:27-38). In Matthew 22:37-40, Jesus says that all the law and all the prophets depend on the commandments to love God and to love our neighbor. To the church at Rome, Paul wrote,

> Owe no one anything, except to love one another; for he who loves his neighbor has fulfilled the law. The commandments, "You shall not commit adultery, You shall not kill, You shall not steal, You shall not covet," and any other commandment, are summed up in this sentence, "You shall love your neighbor as yourself." Love does no wrong to a neighbor; therefore, love is the fulfilling of the law. (Romans 13:8-10)

Paul's beautiful dissertation on love in 1 Corinthians 13 tells us that love is the greatest virtue. He concludes with the statement "So faith, hope, love abide, these three; but the greatest of these is love" (1 Corinthians 13:13). Colossians 3:14 says, "And above all these put on love, which binds everything together in perfect harmony." 1 Peter 4:8 goes so far as to say that "love covers a multitude of sins." Proverbs 10:12 says, "Love covers all offenses." As Paul tells us, even though we may have the gifts of tongues, prophecy, and knowledge, even though we may have mountain-moving faith, if we don't have love, we are nothing but noisy gongs or clanging cymbals (1 Corinthians 13:1-3). We should earnestly desire the spiritual gifts, but we should make love our aim (1 Corinthians 14:1). In essence, love is the bottom line, the litmus test of Christianity.

The Necessity of Works

Jesus' sacrifice on Calvary was essential to our salvation, but I don't think that we can say works have absolutely nothing to do with salvation. In John 15:8, Jesus says that we prove we are His disciples by bearing much fruit. James 1:22-27 says that if we are only hearers of the Word and not doers, we are simply deceiving ourselves. We are not saved by good works, but if we don't do good works, we are not saved. In other words, we don't earn our way into heaven by good works, but works are essential as evidence of our salvation. The following verses are illustrative:

> And he said to them, "Take heed what you hear; the measure you give will be the measure you get, and still more will be given you. For to him who has will more be given; and from him who has not, even what he has will be taken away." (Mark 4:24-25)

> Every one who comes to me and hears my words and does them, I will show you what he is like: he is like a man building a house, who dug deep, and laid the foundation upon rock; and when a flood arose, the stream broke against that house, and could not shake it, because it had been well built. But he who hears and does not do them is like a man who built a house on the ground without a foundation; against which the stream broke, and immediately it fell, and the ruin of that house was great. (Luke 6:47-49)

> Do not marvel at this; for the hour is coming when all who are in the tombs will hear his voice and come forth, those who have done good, to the resurrection of life, and those who have done evil, to the resurrection of judgment. (John 5:28-29)

> Truly, truly, I say to you, he who believes in me will also do the works that I do; and greater works than these will he do, because I go to the Father. (John 14:12)

And being made perfect he became the source of eternal salvation to all who obey him. (Hebrews 5:9)

For you have need of endurance, so that you may do the will of God and receive what is promised. (Hebrews 10:36)

He who says "I know him" but disobeys his commandments is a liar, and the truth is not in him. (1 John 2:4)

By this it may be seen who are the children of God, and who are the children of the devil: Whoever does not do right is not of God, nor he who does not love his brother. (1 John 3:10)

But if anyone has the world's goods and sees his brother in need, yet closes his heart against him, how does God's love abide in him? (1 John 3:17)

All who keep his commandments abide in him, and he in them. And by this we know that he abides in us, by the Spirit which he has given us. (1 John 3:24)

Those Who Have Not Heard

One question that often comes up when discussing the Christian view of salvation is what happens to those who have not heard of Jesus. I don't know. But I do know our God is infinitely loving and infinitely merciful. I sincerely believe that everyone will have an opportunity somehow, somewhere to accept Jesus Christ.

Paul tells us in Romans 9:25-26, "As indeed he says in Hosea, 'Those who were not my people I will call my people, and her who was not my beloved I will call my beloved.' And in the very place where it was said to them 'You are not my people,' they will be called 'sons of the living God.'" Again in Romans 10:20, Paul says, "Then Isaiah is so bold as to say 'I have been found by those who did not ask for me.'" John 15:16 says, "You did not choose me, but I chose you." 1 John 4:10 says, "In this is love, not that we loved God but that he loved us and sent his Son to be the expiation for our sins." And finally, 2 Peter 3:9 tells us that

God is not willing that any should perish, but that all should reach repentance. Suffice it to say, no one will be in hell unless they deserve to be there.

Conclusion

So when all is said and done, is it worth it to be a Christian? Absolutely! Consider the alternatives. We can live Christian lives for our brief time here on earth and spend the rest of eternity with God in the most wonderful place imaginable; a place of perfect love, joy, and peace. Or we can live self-centered, materialistic, sinful lives for our brief time on earth and spend the rest of eternity in the most terrible place imaginable. As Jesus puts it so well in Mark 8:36, "For what does it profit a man, to gain the whole world and forfeit his life." Don't labor for the food which perishes; but for the food that endures to eternal life—namely, Jesus (John 6:27). Heaven is the hidden treasure worth everything we have (Matthew 13:44); it is the pearl of such great value that once we find it, we should be willing to give up everything to get it (Matthew 13:45-46). Heaven is the great banquet to which we've all been invited (Luke 14:16-24).

Being a Christian doesn't mean you can't enjoy this life. I believe the Christian life carries its own rewards here on earth. I think committed Christians tend to be much happier and more satisfied, fulfilled, and at peace than self-centered, materialistic people who are living only for themselves and the things of this world. I think there are a lot of rich, materialistic people who are downright miserable. Being a Christian doesn't mean you can't have fun. I think most Christians have lots of fun. They tend to find enjoyment in the simple things of life like family activities, the beauty of creation, spiritual activities, and relationships. Being a Christian doesn't mean you can't have possessions; but it does mean we can't let our possessions be our focus. We need to keep things in the proper perspective.

The point of this chapter hasn't been to condemn anyone or lay a guilt trip on anyone. John 3:17 tells us "For God sent the Son into the world, not to condemn the world, but that the world might be saved through him." None of us lives up to the ideals of the Gospel 100% of the time; but we have to make a sincere commitment to try. We should maintain a balanced view of salvation, focusing not just on the grace and mercy of God but on doing our part as well. I think that's the Catholic view in a nutshell. As Psalm 119:166 puts it succinctly; we need to hope for the Lord's salvation, but also do his commandments. We should live, as Paul puts it, as citizens of heaven (Philippians 3:20), not as citizens of this world. Heaven is our home; we're just temporarily residing here. So as an old folk song says, "keep your eyes on the prize and hold on."

"For every one who calls upon the name of the Lord will be saved." (Romans 10:13)

CHAPTER III

History

Not My Favorite Subject

Let me preface this chapter by stating that history was never my favorite or best subject. I agree with Isaiah 43:18-19: "Remember not the former things, nor consider the things of old. Behold, I am doing a new thing; now it springs forth, do you not perceive it? I will make a way in the wilderness and rivers in the desert." To me, the important thing is not where we were a thousand years ago, but where we are today and where we are heading.

Church history has some good and some bad. Like any history, it tends to focus on the major events in the life of the institution, whereas God focuses on the lives of the individual church members. Church history focuses on the splits, the schisms, the power struggles, the scandals, the inquisitions, etc. rather than the changed lives, the answered prayers, the miracles, the sacrifices, and the service and dedication of countless human beings who found salvation in Jesus Christ. I suppose it is human nature to focus on negative events rather than positive. When we pick up the newspaper we don't read about good, hard-working, God-fearing people; we read about the murderers, the frauds, the phonies, the con artists, etc.

Despite this, I feel it is important to know something about the history of the Catholic Church in order to understand its development, its philosophy, and even its theology. To understand its history, we must, in turn, understand something of the corresponding political, social, economic, and philosophical trends, influences, and pressures of the times. Why did we have crusades and inquisitions? Why did the Church at one time chain the Bible and resist its translation into the common languages and its distribution among the common people? How did various superstitions creep into the Church? How could practices like the selling of indulgences and simony (the selling of Church offices) happen? How did the doctrine of papal infallibility develop? What factors led to the Protestant Reformation?

These are the questions I hope to answer in this chapter. The history of the Catholic Church is, to a great extent, a history of struggle: struggle against heresies; struggle with monarchies, dictatorships, and various political systems; struggle with persecution; struggle for its very survival. No wonder the Church was so concerned about the efforts of reformers who might weaken or impair its authority and unity.

Reading Church history is a little like reading the Old Testament. The Hebrew people went through times of worldliness and backsliding. They got into idol worship. They intermingled with heathens. They strayed from the Word of God. They grumbled and murmured. They broke the commandments. They had some bad leaders. They killed some of their own prophets. Time and time again God became angry with them. But time and time again, he remembered his covenant, forgave them, and called them back. They were still God's people. And even in the midst of their most sinful times, the Word of God was still proclaimed by the prophets to a sinful and rebellious people. Likewise, in the history of the Catholic Church, we have had our saints and our sinners, our good leaders and our not-so-good leaders, our great accomplishments and our failures.

It is easy for us to look back and criticize and say how unenlightened people were "back then;" but what will people say about the twentieth and twenty-first centuries 400 years from now? Couldn't they say how cruel, how barbaric, how un-Christian we were? How we turned away from God? How the media glorified immoral behavior while ridiculing religion? How God and religion were systematically excluded from our public life? Couldn't they criticize the cruel dictatorships, the two world wars and numerous smaller wars, political leaders using chemical weapons on their own people, the use of nuclear weapons for the first time? Our destruction of the environment, destruction of the family unit, corruption in government, corruption in the Body of Christ, people preaching for material gain? How we ignored the needs of the poor and homeless? Widespread involvement in the ancient practices of witchcraft and the occult, people actually worshiping Satan? The lowering of educational standards, the increase in illiteracy, the widespread drug and alcohol addiction, the millions of abortions, the dramatic increase in divorce rates, apartheid? Couldn't they honestly look back and say that the twentieth and twenty-first centuries were really the Dark Ages?

It is obviously a formidable task to cover 2,000 years of Church history in a single chapter. Rather than focusing on the details, I will attempt to discuss the general trends within the Church and within society as a whole throughout the ages. Hopefully, this will help us understand not only what happened, but why.

The First Century

After seeing Jesus resurrected from the dead and after receiving the power of the Holy Spirit, nothing could stop the disciples from preaching the Gospel. At first, Christianity was considered a sect of Judaism, but then it was opened up to the Gentiles. Vicious persecution and cruel tortures were inflicted upon Christians by wicked and insane rulers such as Claudius, Nero, Caligula, and Herod Agrippa I. Christians were crucified, burned at the stake, roasted in hot iron chairs, dragged to death by wild bulls, and torn to pieces by wild animals. The reason for the persecutions was that Christians refused to worship the Roman emperor as God. Despite these persecutions, and to some extent because of them, the Church spread rapidly (Acts 2:41). A faith community started to form (Acts 2:42-47).

Joining the Christian faith was thus a life-and-death decision. The converts had to be very sincere to embrace Christianity. The martyrs of the early Church were held in awe and admiration. Their names were carefully kept, and their "birthdays into eternal life" were remembered by annual celebrations. This is the background of the recognition of saints in the Catholic Church.

The persecutions were a great witness to the pagan world. People had to stand up and take notice that Jesus Christ made a dramatic impact on the lives of these Christians. What was it that made these people lead such good and holy lives? Who was this man Jesus, that these people were willing to die rather than renounce him? As Tertullian said, "The blood of martyrs was the seed of Christianity." The Church spread throughout the Roman Empire in places such as Samaria, Damascus, Antioch, Tarsus, and Cyprus in Egypt.

In 64 A.D., Nero burned Rome and blamed it on the Christians. Tradition holds that Peter and Paul were martyred in Rome between 64 and 67 A.D. In 66 A.D., the emperor Vespasian's forces, led by Titus, totally destroyed Jerusalem, thus fulfilling Jesus' prophecy in Matthew

24:2. In the midst of all this turmoil, Christianity offered peace, love, tranquility, and eternal salvation. Starting from the tiny group of twelve apostles, it is estimated that, by the end of the first century, there were half a million Christians.

The Second Century

In addition to the threat of persecution, the Church was threatened by various heresies such as (1) Docetism (the belief that Christ was not really a man but a spirit who only appeared human), (2) Gnosticism (the belief that physical matter was evil; that God didn't create the physical universe. Gnostics believed that the christ could not be human. Thus, the first major test to the Christian faith was not denial of Jesus' deity but rejection of His humanity.); and (3) Ebionites (a Jewish sect that taught that Jesus was a mere man who, by his scrupulous obedience to the law, was "justified" and became the Messiah). Several other "isms" such as Manichaeanism, monarchianism and adoptionism also existed at this time.

In the early second century, the Church started calling itself Catholic, meaning "universal." Ignatius, Bishop of Antioch, was apparently the first to use the word. The Catholic Church was both universal (as opposed to local congregations) and orthodox (in contrast to the many heretical groups).

Several important early Christian writers, beginning with Irenaeus in the second century, referred to Peter and Paul as founders of the Church in Rome and to subsequent bishops as successors of the apostles. The Church in Rome rose in its prestige and preeminence. Descriptions of the Mass (originally called the Lord's Supper) go all the way back to the writings of Justin Martyr (d. 165 A.D.).

Despite widespread and determined efforts to eliminate Christianity, it survived and grew. Persecutions and martyrdoms helped to publicize the new Christian faith. These events were often held in the amphitheater and were witnessed by thousands. By the end of second century the number of Christians had grown to about two million.

The Third Century

From 200 A.D. onward, persecution of the Christian Church became even more widespread and systematic. There were mass persecutions and assaults on the Church's organization. The Roman Empire was threatened by Germanic tribes, and it began blaming its problems on Christianity and the decline of the Roman pagan religion. The Christian religion was declared harmful to the Roman Empire and was forbidden.

Despite these problems, the Church continued to grow. By the end of the third century there were some five million Christians. Christian liturgy also developed. The Church Order of Hippolytus (d. 236) shows that the Eucharistic prayer at that time was very similar to those used today.

The Fourth Century

As the fourth century began, the vicious persecution of Christians continued. By a decree of February 303, Diocletian ordered all Christian places of worship to be destroyed and their sacred books handed over. Christians were forbidden to assemble and were denied the protection of the laws. Bishops, priests, and deacons were given especially severe treatment. Later, great numbers of Christians in all ranks were seized. They had their eyes and tongues gouged out, their feet sawed off; they died at the stake or in red-hot chairs. Some were thrown to wild beasts to entertain holiday crowds.

When the Emperor Constantine rose to power, however, the situation suddenly changed. Constantine is one of the major figures of Christian history. He was sympathetic to Christianity and stopped the persecution of Christians. In 313 A.D., Constantine made Christianity legal by the Edict of Milan. After Constantine's conversion, Christianity moved swiftly from the seclusion of the catacombs to the prestige of palaces. Constantine was very generous toward the Church and erected numerous sumptuous basilicas. He gave his palace to the Bishop of Rome and moved his residence to Byzantium, changing the city's name to Constantinople in 330 A.D. The Bishop of Constantinople came to take precedence immediately after the Bishop of Rome. Constantinople was considered the "new Rome."

Constantine bestowed important privileges on the Christian clergy. They were recognized as a distinct social class. Bishops were given some civil and judicial authority. As a result of this special status accorded to the clergy, however, the gap between clergy and laity was widened. The clergy began to identify more with nobility.

Church architecture under Constantine became splendid, public and imposing. Constantine reigned from 312 to 337 A.D. During his reign churches were built in every large town in the empire and in places as distant from each other as Britain, Carthage, and Persia. What had begun as a tiny offshoot of Judaism three centuries later became the favorite and, eventually, official religion of the Roman Empire.

The Emperor Theodosius (379-395) declared Christianity to be the religion of all the people in the Roman Empire in his Edict of 380. His decree also outlawed paganism. Belief in Christianity was a matter of "imperial demand." Nonbelievers were declared "demented and insane." Penalties were imposed for non-Christians. The Roman Empire thus went from one extreme (persecution of Christians) to the other (persecution of non-Christians). Church and State were officially united. This union came to be known as "Christendom." The Roman Empire became the "Holy Roman Empire," a title that was not always deserved.

The union of Church and State brought both benefits and burdens to the Church. Obviously, the freedom to profess and practice Christian beliefs without fear of persecution was a tremendous blessing. Another benefit was the influence that Christianity had on Roman law, which had previously allowed abortion, abandonment of children, and infanticide. Through Christian influence, these crimes were outlawed. Divorce was consistently condemned in the Church, in keeping with the teachings of Jesus.

But the blessings of the State had political strings attached. The marriage of Church and State was a quarrelsome one. Civil authorities often exploited the relationship for political purposes. Constantine ruled Christian bishops just as he did civil servants. He demanded unconditional obedience to official pronouncements, even when they interfered with purely Church matters. Again and again, Constantine and his successors stepped in to banish or exile churchmen as they saw fit. Control of Church offices too often depended on control of the emperor's favor.

Another mixed blessing to the Church was the mass conversion of millions of pagans. The masses quickly adopted the Christian religion, but not necessarily for the right reasons. The religion of the political leader was the religion of the people; it was as simple as that. This led to influences of secularization and misuse of religion for political purposes.

Thus, the Church was confronted with a general decline in Christian sincerity and commitment. The stalwart believers whom Diocletion killed were replaced by a mixed multitude of half-converted pagans. These "converts" brought with them a number of pagan practices and superstitions. Rather than outlawing these practices altogether, the Church tried to "Christianize" them. Thus, the practice of kissing pagan objects as a sign of reverence was transferred to kissing holy objects. The practice of genuflection was adopted as reverence to Jesus in the Blessed Sacrament. Pagan holidays became Christian feast days, celebrating events in Christian history. For example, Epiphany (January 6) took the place of the pagan festival celebrating the birth of the New Year. Christmas (December 25) coincided with the birthday of the sun. The Church simply changed "sun" to "Son."

Although the doctrine of separation of Church and State can be taken to ridiculous extremes, Christendom proves that there are some benefits to it. When the power of the State is used in the name of religion, the results can be catastrophic. Inquisitions and crusades—the use of force to suppress religious opposition—date back to Constantine. After his conversion, the policy of using force against heretics began.

One of the most significant events of the fourth century was the Council of Nicea, called by Constantine in 325, in which the Nicene Creed was adopted. In one simple prayer, several false doctrines were dispelled and the basic Christian faith was stated. The struggle with Arianism was settled quickly—Jesus is true God of true God; begotten, not made; of one substance with the Father. This was an extremely important matter because, in effect, Arianism questioned the most basic tenet of the Christian faith—the Divinity of Christ. To this day, the Nicene Creed is the standard of orthodoxy in the Roman, Eastern, Anglican, and some other Christian churches. It is essentially the same as the creed we say at Mass today.

On the positive side, the fourth century was a time of great accomplishments in the Christian faith. It was during this century that St. Jerome (340-420 A.D.) translated the Bible into Latin. Jerome, a great Scripture scholar, studied Hebrew until he mastered it. At the behest of Pope Damascus (d. 384), he undertook the work of translating the Bible from the original languages. Until that time, the only translation was based on the Greek Septuagint translation. Jerome went back to the original Hebrew. The work took him more than 20 years. The new translation by Jerome was called the Latin Vulgate. It was an excellent translation and was used by the Catholic Church until recent years.

About the same time that Jerome was creating the Latin Vulgate, however, a missionary named Ulifilis (or Wulfila) converted the Visigoths to Arianism. The Ostrogoths and Vandals were also Arians. Wulfila translated the Bible into the Gothic language, with the exception of select portions he didn't like. This was the danger the Church saw in allowing the Bible to be translated into common languages. It would be too susceptible to mistranslation, misinterpretation, additions, deletions, and cultic influences. No wonder the Church became so protective of the sacred Scriptures. Can you imagine a Bible translated by someone like Attila the Hun?

St. Augustine also lived in the fourth century (354-430). Like Paul, Augustine had a dramatic conversion. He sensed profoundly the greatness of his sin and of God's mercy. He recognized that salvation was by divine grace and only constantly inflowing grace could keep him in the Christian life. To St. Augustine, the Christian ideal wasn't stoic self-control but love for righteousness infused by the Spirit of God. Augustine became a great philosopher. His works on the grace and mercy of God are classic.

Another saint of the fourth century was St. Ambrose, noted for his eloquent and intelligent interpretations of Scripture. St. Ambrose had a confrontation with Emperor Theodosius that would prove extremely significant in the relationship between Church and State in years to come. Theodosius got in trouble with the Church when he mercilessly slaughtered about 7,000 Thessalonians for an uprising in which the governor was killed. Ambrose took the daring step of refusing the emperor communion until he would confess his sin and repent. Finally, Theodosius gave in and did what Ambrose said. Ambrose had hit upon the one weapon—the threat of excommunication—that the Church would use over and over to humble monarchs.

As a reaction to the secularization influence, monasticism began to grow. Sincere Christians began to sing the praises of self-denial, especially of celibacy. Many believers took vows of abstinence. Eventually, they began withdrawing from ordinary life in the cities. Their aim was the imitation of Christ and to live only for God. To help them do this, they assumed vows of poverty, chastity, and obedience. The monastic call became a call to study. The monks became scholars. The Benedictine monks read and copied the great Christian works of Latin antiquity and thus preserved them for us. Jerome was the pioneer of Monastic worship.

In summary, the fourth century was a century of profound impact on the history of Christianity and the Roman Catholic Church.

The Fifth Century

Why did the Church become so involved in politics? Why did the papacy become so strong? The fifth century gives us some clues.

In the fifth century, the Roman Empire was under attack from all sides by various barbarian groups. The Church was part of an establishment that was collapsing. In 410 A.D., Rome was sacked by the Visigoths. In 455, it was sacked by the Vandals. The year 476 marked the end of the Western Roman Empire. What would become of the Church?

The Barbarians did not embrace Christianity. The Goths and Vandals were Arians and they persecuted Catholics whenever they took over. In the midst of all this turmoil, Pope Leo assumed the papacy. Leo was a strong leader who saw the need for a strong papacy. There had to be one chief executive officer, one president so to speak, of the Catholic Church. There had to be one place where the buck would stop and where the decisions would be final. That leader would be the pope.

Pope Leo stood up to Attila the Hun in 452 A.D. and persuaded him to spare Rome from destruction. A few years later, he stood up to Gaiseric the Vandal. Gaiseric did not turn aside, but at Leo's insistence, limited himself to a "peaceful sack." On the doctrinal side, Leo faced the old controversy over the relationship of Christ's humanity to his divinity. Leo resolved it clearly and concisely: Jesus was fully human and fully divine, and that was it.

The Church had to work to convert the Barbarians and to establish diplomatic relations with them in order to survive and prevent the establishment of Arianism. When Clovis, ruler of the Salian Franks, married a Catholic, he and 3,000 of his men were baptized. He overthrew the Vandals and Goths and established Catholic Christianity in the areas he conquered.

Thus, Rome fell but the Church and papacy survived. Rather than giving up, the Church undertook the evangelistic effort of converting the Barbarians. The papacy grew in power and influence under Pope Leo the Great.

The Sixth and Seventh Centuries

The Church was threatened by the savage Lombards, who burned churches, killed bishops, robbed monasteries, and reduced cultivated fields to wilderness. Pope Gregory the Great saved Rome from sack several times by diplomatic maneuvers and finally led the way in establishing peace. Gregory called himself simply "servant of the servants of God." He paved the way for conversion of the Lombards by his diplomacy and his close friendship with Theodolinda, Queen of two successive Lombard rulers, Authari and Agiluluf. The monks were also effective in missionary activity with their monasteries located throughout the countryside.

With the alliance of the Franks and the papacy, Christendom (the union of Church and State) was again established, along with its familiar problems. Who would be the final authority—pope or emperor? Church or State? Would the pope have the right to intervene in the affairs of the State? Would the king have the right to intervene in the affairs of the Church?

Another continuing problem with Christendom was the mass conversions. When the king embraced the faith, his subjects followed him. But the conversions were not always sincere, and the converts brought with them their superstitions and practices.

Gregory was a powerful and diplomatic leader. On the doctrinal side, he emphasized belief in the intercession of the saints and the custom of appealing to them to intercede for us. He also emphasized the real presence of Christ in the Eucharist.

The Eighth Century

On the political side, in 754 A.D., a portion of Italy was designated as the pope's realm. The pope became a temporal ruler as well as a spiritual leader in this area. This set the stage for power struggles that plagued the Church for many years. The Church became a civil institution as well as a spiritual one.

On the doctrinal side, a controversy arose over the Eastern Church's use of holy images, or "icons." These were considered to be sacred, inspired paintings. Some Christians, however, failed to make the distinction between the object and the person it represented, and they began to worship the icon. Emperor Leo III (717-741) launched an attack on icons as idolatry. The iconoclast (image breaker) movement gained momentum. The iconoclasts wanted to replace the religious icons with traditional Christian symbols such as the cross and the Bible.

John Mansour (730-760), better known as John of Damascus, gave the explanation recognized today in Orthodox churches for the use of icons. Although it was wrong to *worship* an icon, the presence of an icon of Christ, Mary, the apostles, the saints, and even the angels could inspire and assist the believer in the worship of Jesus Christ. But the icon itself was only a reminder to help the faithful give proper respect and reverence to the Lord.

The Ninth Century

The pope crowned Charles the Great (Charlemagne), king of the Franks, in 800 A.D. This act of homage by the pope restored the Christian Roman Empire and gave the Church a powerful protector against the Lombards. Although this union led to rivalry between the pope and the king, it helped preserve the survival of Christianity, or so it was thought. The alliance between the pope and Charlemagne was pragmatic. The pope needed protection; Charlemagne needed divine sanction.

Charlemagne conquered the Bavarians and Saxons, divided Saxony into districts called bishoprics, built monasteries, and proclaimed harsh laws against paganism. Eating meat during Lent, cremating the dead and pretending to be baptized became offenses punishable by death. Again we see the danger of uniting Church and State and of civil rulers making religious laws.

Charlemagne's protection didn't last long. Once he left the scene, his successors were too weak and the empire too vast to hold everything together. The empire disintegrated with civil wars and Viking invasions. The Viking Magyar invaders brought anarchy and carried Europe into the age of feudalism, a type of government in which political power was exercised locally by private individuals rather than a centralized state.

The prospect of the complete ruin of Christian society became a very real threat in the Dark Ages that followed. It was an age of lawlessness, rationalization, destruction, oppression, and violence. The papacy declined in power and prestige. The Church was caught in the middle of a collapsed society that it could no longer control. Emperors even deposed popes and had laymen installed in their place (for example, Otto and John XII). In the Ottonian Empire, the popes, like the bishops, were nominees and lieutenants of the temporal sovereign. The emperors employed bishops as officials and made and unmade popes as they saw fit.

Throughout Europe, local feudal potentates used and abused the Church. Through the ceremony of lay investiture, local feudal lords selected and installed bishops who knelt before the lord and rendered him homage and fealty. The bishop usually had to pay a heavy fee for his promotion. Bishops, in turn, resorted to simony (commerce in spiritual matters) to support themselves. The criteria set forth in 1 Timothy 3:1-7 often had little to do with the appointment of these bishops. Thus, the quality and morality of some of the Church leaders declined, not from within the Church but as a result of outside political corruption. This decline is not a reflection of failure on the part of the Church but a failure on the part of feudalism. The result, however, is that the Church was blamed for the bad popes and bishops.

The Tenth Century

The Cluniac Reform Movement begun by the Benedictine Order in 910 sought to do away with simony (the purchase and sale of church offices) and to free the Church from secular control and subject it to papal authority. The German king, Otto, revived the Roman Empire in the west in 962, and some sense of unity was restored. Renewal of the empire, of course, brought with it the old rivalry between Church and State. The German tribes continuously interfered in ecclesiastical affairs. The union of Church and State also led to crusades, inquisitions, and persecution of "heretics." As abhorrent as this was, the Old Testament reveals that religious wars and the persecution of heretics are nothing new.

The Church had fought long and hard for its survival, and it was not about to allow the questioning of its authority or doctrines. The Church was very protective of the Bible and would not allow any unauthorized translations. It feared the formation of numerous sects, each claiming to be the true church, so that eventually no one would know what to believe. The Church was concerned about what would happen if semiliterate lay people got their hands on loose translations of the Bible and started interpreting it for themselves. In retrospect, the Church's concerns may have been somewhat justified. Do we really need some 300 different denominations and 27 translations of the Bible?

The Eleventh Century

The Middle Ages—the eleventh to fourteenth centuries—were a time of contradictions. It was a time of intellectual revolution in art, philosophy, theology, modes of worship, and piety; but it was also a time of barbaric terror and death, superstition and witchcraft. Political rulers used crusades (holy wars) as excuses to conquer foreign lands. It was done in the name of spreading the Gospel, but the motives were really political.

The Church had become a rich and powerful institution, identified with the establishment. Bishops, priests, monks, friars, and nuns were the most educated and respected members of medieval society. The clergy were the spiritual elite. The masses were illiterate, and the clergy worked to instill faith in them and educate them about Christian principles, morals, and values. The Church's theologians worked out an ethical system to provide answers for every conceivable moral question. It based these principles on Scriptures, "natural law" (human reason), and the authority of the Church.

On the positive side, from the tenth to fourteenth centuries, universities were established to provide education and spread the faith. New religious orders were founded by great spiritual leaders like St. Francis of Assisi (Franciscans) and St. Dominic (Dominicans). The Renaissance Age brought intellectual challenges to the Church; but great Christian philosophers like Thomas Aquinas responded by harmonizing faith and reason. Aquinas applied Aristotelian logic to the Gospel. The Church also had noted scholars in astronomy, mathematics, physics, optics, and scientific invention, such as Robert Grosseteste, bishop of Lincoln, and Franciscan scholar Roger Bacon. Other great Church philosophers who embraced intellectualism rather than fleeing from it included two Dominicans—Bonaventure and Albert the Great—and another Franciscan, John Duns Scotus.

The papacy itself became a monarchy of sorts, with pronouncements of Papal authority that seem incongruous to the Vatican II Church of today. One must keep in mind that these pronouncements and Papal titles date back to the eleventh century. It was a troubled time for the Church. There was a vital need for the Church to have one powerful, authoritative ruler to hold it together against various competing viewpoints and fractions. It was not a time for compromise and collegiality. The world was on the brink of anarchy. Papal monarchy protected the local churches from the tyranny of a local bishop or lord. The Church was threatened with splits from within and political domination without.

During the eleventh century, the controversy between Church and State centered on the issue of lay investiture. There were critics in the Church such as Cardinal Humbert who denounced simony and lay investiture. Before those evils could be overcome, however, the papacy itself had to be liberated from the iron grip of the emperor. That chance occurred when Emperor Henry III died and left only a six-year-old to succeed him (1056 A.D.). The Roman Curia seized control of the papacy and installed Stephen IX; and when Stephen soon died, they elected Nicholas II (d. 1061). In 1059, an epoch-making decree was issued, formally excluding the emperor and the riotous Roman nobles from taking part in papal elections. Henceforth, only the cardinals would elect the pope, although some type of confirmation was allowed to the emperor.

Pope Gregory VII, elected in 1073, finally had the courage and strength to bring an end to lay investiture by decree in 1075. King Henry IV challenged the decree and called Gregory a false pope. Gregory responded by excommunicating him. The excommunication was devastating to Henry. He lost his supporters while his enemies rallied against him. Henry finally repented, yielded to the pope, and stood barefoot in the snow for three days until the pope granted him absolution.

The first schism in the Church occurred in 1054 between Roman Catholics and Eastern Orthodox. It was due more to cultural and political differences than doctrinal differences and was precipitated by Leo IX excommunicating the patriarch of Constantinople, Michael Cerularius.

The Twelfth Century

The Middle Ages were not all dark. Between 1170 and 1270, more than 500 great churches (including Notre Dame Cathedral) were built in Gothic style in France alone. The Church took the lead in rule by law, the pursuit of knowledge, and the expressions of culture. It was Christianity that brought life and order out of chaos.

The problem of lay investiture was finally settled in 1122 by the compromise known as the Concordat of Worms. The Church maintained the right to elect the holder of an ecclesiastical office, but only in the presence of the emperor or his representative. The papacy continued to grow in power until people began to think of the popes as world leaders. The pope's most powerful weapon was the threat of excommunication. While under excommunication, people could not act as judge, juror, witness, or attorney. They could not be guardians, executors, or parties to a contract; and after death, they received no Christian burial.

On the negative side, the union of Church and State continued to give the State the authority and power to punish heretics, confiscate their property, and excommunicate those who would not move against a heretic. Inquisitions began in 1184, and crusades were fought between 1100 and 1300 A.D.

The Thirteenth Century

The period from 1300 to 1500 A.D. is referred to as "The Decline of the Middle Ages." Christendom was under attack, and papal prestige declined. European Christians no longer accepted papal interference in what they regarded as purely political matters. In the long run, this was probably good.

On the positive side, education was on the rise in the thirteenth century. Thomas Aquinas was the great Church scholar of the age. St. Francis of Assisi began a movement back to simple basic Christianity, living out the Gospel and giving up the material things of this world. On the negative side, the thirteenth century was a time of horrible political rulers such as Frederick Hohenstafen, King of Sicily from 1211 to 1250. Frederick was deceitful, cruel, sensual, and bizarre. He sought to dominate the Church and posed a serious threat to the papacy. Frederick became paranoid of imaginary papal assassins and conspirators and had many people tortured in barbaric ways such as being blinded with red-hot irons, dragged to death by horses over stony ground, and sewn up in leather sacks with poisonous snakes and tossed into the sea.

In the face of such threats, it is no wonder that the popes fought back with spiritual weapons. Gregory IX excommunicated Frederick. The popes sought to keep Sicily under papal rule. Horrible accusations were hurled at popes by civil rulers. Papal prestige, authority, and esteem declined. Finally, the papacy was forced to flee to Avignon.

The scandal of the papacy's 70-year absence from Rome was followed by the incredible disaster of the 40-year great schism, when two and eventually three popes fought each other for control of the Church. Each pope threatened to excommunicate those who did not acknowledge him. Pope Urban VI was one of the worst. He ruled from Rome while Clement ruled from Avignon. This was probably the darkest hour in Catholic Church history.

The Fourteenth Century

Different civil governments backed different popes, splitting Christendom into various camps. France, Scotland, Luxembourg, and Austria supported Clement. Other countries supported Urban. Urban was not a good pope. Neither was John XXIII (the first one). It is significant that the pope who ushered in Vatican II chose the same name, as if to replace the first John XXIII.

The first Protestant reformer arrived on the scene in the fourteenth century—the English zealot, John Wycliffe. He believed the Church was divided into three parts—one triumphant in heaven, one militant here on earth, and one asleep in purgatory. He believed strongly in predestination. Images were allowable, provided they increased devotion. Prayers to the saints were not necessarily wrong, and confession was useful, provided it was voluntary.

The Fifteenth and Sixteenth Centuries

The Church from its beginning has been beset by crisis: persecution, heresies, Church-State struggles, barbarian invasions, and the like. But the fifteenth and sixteenth centuries brought the greatest crisis— the Protestant Reformation. Various religious groups under individual leaders split over issues of reform and doctrine. There was a mass exodus of people from the Church, including many nuns and priests. By the time it was over, half of Europe had left the Roman Catholic Church. The unity of Christendom was gone. The new branch of Christianity called "Protestant" included Lutheranism, Calvinism, Anglicanism, Anabaptistism, and radical Protestantism.

There was, no doubt, a need for reform in the Church. The Church had become contaminated by superstition, "magic," and corruption. There were scandals and abuses such as the selling of indulgences and dispensations by some unscrupulous members of the clergy. As bad as this was, I cannot help but notice that some of the current preachers who are quick to condemn the Catholic Church for practices that occurred hundreds of years ago are basically doing the same thing themselves. They may not call it selling indulgences, but they get on television and say things like "If you give me $100, God will give you $1,000. If you send me money, we will pray that God will bless you. We will believe God for a miracle in your life." They may condemn the ancient practice of simony (selling church offices) and yet tell people that for "X" number of dollars they can be basic members of the ministry and receive certain materials. For "X"-plus- "Y" dollars they can be champion members, or whatever. It seems to me that some of these ministries come very close to selling memberships.

Most Catholic leaders realized the need for reform. But realizing the need and getting everyone to agree on what should be done were two different things. After years of conflict between popes, emperors, and anti-popes, the papacy was threatened and had lost much of its prestige. In 1409, the cardinals met, deposed both papal claimants (Urban and Clement) and elected a third man, Alexander V. The first John XXIII was finally tried and deposed. Many Catholic leaders, such as Ignatius Loyola and Thomas More, pursued reform vigorously; but the papacy did not respond quickly or positively enough.

The first major reformer was Martin Luther (1483-1546). He confronted the scandals and superstitions in the Church head on. These issues could have and should have been addressed within the Church itself; but instead of agreeing to meet with Luther to resolve the issues on scriptural and theological grounds, the Church hierarchy scorned and rebuked him. Pope Leo X basically ignored Luther and showed no inclination to dialogue. From a theological standpoint, Luther's central doctrine of justification by faith wasn't that far from the Catholic position. Luther was an Augustinian monk and was greatly influenced by St. Augustine's works, which emphasized God's grace and mercy. In fact, his position on salvation was in accordance with that of Thomas Aquinas (see *"Luther and Aquinas on Salvation"* by S. Pfurtner; New York: Sheed and Ward, 1964).

Luther translated the Bible and the liturgy into the language of the people. These reforms were eventually adopted by the Catholic Church as well. If Luther and the Church could have gotten together for honest, prayerful discussion, the split probably could have been avoided. As late as 1519 Martin Luther said, "I never liked the idea of dividing the Church and never will."[1]

Not long after the initial Reformation, the Protestants began splitting off from each other. The first split was between Luther and Zwingli (1484-1556). Zwingli did not agree with Luther or the Catholic position on the presence of Jesus in communion. He believed the bread and wine were mere memorials of Jesus. Zwingli was the pioneer of Puritanism. Next came John Calvin. He disagreed with Luther over the Lord's Supper, the canon of Scripture, the sacraments and the importance of living a life of holiness.

Calvin was a scholar and a lawyer. He basically agreed with the Catholic position on original sin. He agreed that Jesus is one with the Father and the Holy Spirit and that He is fully human and fully divine. He agreed that Jesus was really present in the Eucharist and that the bread and wine are instruments by which Jesus distributes his body and blood to us. Calvin's worship service, although simplified, followed the basic outline of the Mass. Where the Church really parted company with Calvin was on the issue of predestination. Calvin strongly emphasized the belief that some are infallibly predestined for eternal life and others for eternal punishment. Catholics believe that God is infinitely merciful, infinitely loving, and infinitely just; and that He wants everyone to be saved (2 Peter 3:9). How could a God who loved us enough to send His only son to the cross for our salvation predestine anyone to eternal torment in hell? Catholics believe very strongly in the concept of free will. We control our eternal destinies through our decisions, actions, and beliefs.

Calvin was a very strict disciplinarian. He excommunicated those whose lives didn't conform to his spiritual requirements. Offenses included drinking, gambling, dancing, adultery, and being absent from public worship. Calvin was the civil ruler in Geneva, where Calvinism was the official religion. To be a citizen of Geneva, one had to accept Calvin's confession of faith. Calvinism has since gone through its own splits, leading to the formation of various denominations, including

[1]Alfred Lapple. *The Catholic Church—A Brief History* (translated by Peter Neinegg). Mahwah, NJ: Paulist Press, 1982, p. 52.

Presbyterian, Dutch and German Reformed, and many Baptist and Congregationalist churches.

Anglicanism—the Church of England—traces its beginning to the marital difficulties of King Henry VIII (1509-1547). Henry wanted the pope to annul his marriage to Catherine of Aragon so he could marry Ann Boleyn. When the pope refused, Henry got parliament to enact laws severing England from the pope's jurisdiction and making the king the supreme head of the Church of England. Thus, the initial Reformation in England had little to do with theology. Henry had no problem with Catholic doctrine. In fact, he was opposed to the Reformation ideas and wrote a treatise against Luther. Henry's six articles of 1539 upheld Catholic articles such as clerical celibacy, the Mass, and confession to a priest. Two major changes under Henry, however, were suppression of the monasteries and publication of the English Bible.

The Calvinist movement eventually broke out in England under the name "Puritanism." Puritans stripped away more traditional symbols of the Catholic Church such as candles, statues, music, and pictures. They required a decisive commitment to Jesus Christ expressed in the public arena. Puritanism was the taproot of Evangelical Christianity, with its born-again emphasis. It was from the Puritans via King James I of England that we got the King James version of the Bible. In America, the Puritans founded commonwealths based on Calvinist doctrine and governed by the truths of the Bible.

Anabaptism was another reform. Sometimes referred to as "radical discipleship," Anabaptism called the moderate reformers to strike even more deeply at the old order. Its primary emphasis was on separation of Church and State. Anabaptists refused to be part of worldly power, including the bearing of arms, holding political office, and taking oaths. In contrast, the Catholic Church encourages involvement in the political system to promote Christian values, social and economic justice, and family concerns. The opposite agenda is being vigorously pursued and the Church can't afford to sit back and watch. Today the Anabaptists are the Mennonites and Hutterites. Distant relatives of the Anabaptists would include Baptists, Quakers, and, to some extent, Congregationalists.

One could argue that the reformers exhibited some of the same intolerance they attributed to the Church. For example, in a treatise published in 1545, Martin Luther wrote, "They should take the pope, the cardinals and all the rabble serving his idolatry and papal holiness and rip their tongues right out of their mouths, as blasphemers against God, and then hang them one after the other on the gallows."[2] In Germany, Luther gained the support of the nobles and took their side when the peasants revolted. In a pamphlet titled "Against the Thievish and Murderous Hordes of Peasants," he encouraged the nobles to knock down, strangle, and stab the peasants, and referred to them as venomous, pernicious, and satanic.[3] The nobles crushed the revolt in 1525, at the cost of about 100,000 peasant lives. The peasants considered Luther a false prophet, and many of them returned to Catholicism or other forms of Christianity arising from the Reformation.

Time magazine once wrote of Luther that "He endorsed the bigamous marriage of his supporter Prince Philip of Hesse. He denounced reformers who disagreed with him in terms that he had once reserved for the papacy. His statements about Jews would sound excessive on the tongue of a Hitler." By the time of his death in 1546, says biographer Roland Binton, Luther was "an irascible old man, petulant, peevish, unrestrained and at times positively coarse."[4]

Calvin, another reformer referred to above, has been accused of ruling Geneva as a dictator. People who opposed him did so at their peril. He had one man (Jacques Gruet) arrested, tortured, and finally beheaded for blasphemy. Another man (Michael Serventes) was burned at the stake for heresy. Generally, Calvin preferred a more merciful death than burning for the heretics, but he did support the silencing of "ill-balanced thinkers." Citizens of Geneva could be brought before the elders and magistrates for even trivial offenses like laughing at a sermon, singing songs defamatory of Calvin, dancing or frequenting a fortune teller. They could be excommunicated by the civil authorities. The penalty for adultery was death.

The English reformer, Henry VIII, dealt severely with those who refused to accept his supremacy over the Church. Thomas More and John Fisher, bishop of Rochester, were beheaded. Henry imposed savage penalties for denial of transubstantiation, private Masses, private

---

[2]Alfred Lapple. *The Catholic Church—A Brief History* (translated by Peter Heinegg). Mahwah, NJ: Paulist Press, 1982, p. 58.

[3]Bruce L. Shelley. *Church History in Plain Language.* Waco, TX: Word Books, 1982, p. 261.

[4]Shelley, Supra, p. 264.

confessions, or the need for clerical celibacy. He dissolved the monasteries and sent some 9,000 nuns and monks packing. An enormous amount of wealth and property was thus acquired.

Anabaptism had its fanatics too. In 1534, a former innkeeper, Jan of Leiden, seized the powers of government and ruled as an absolute despot. Claiming new revelations from God, Jan introduced the Old Testament practice of polygamy and took the title "King David."

The Council of Trent (sometimes called the "Counter Reformation") was the Church's response to the Reformation. It clarified Church doctrine on such matters as original sin, the sacraments, and the Mass. It sought to correct shortcomings of the past and to instruct the faithful. Popes Pius V, Gregory XIII, and Sixtus V helped put the Council's decrees into effect. The Council was convened on December 13, 1545 and took 18 years (1545–1563) to complete its work. The "Decree on Justification" proclaimed at the sixth session of the Council was a masterful work. If it had come a bit earlier, Luther's split might never have occurred. The trend of the Council was very conservative but it did restore order of doctrine and practice in the Catholic Church, without which the Church may have disintegrated completely.

The Catechism of the Council of Trent was published by Pope Pius V. It was a clear, concise summary of Catholic beliefs and practices. Also, the Roman Missal was published to ensure that the Roman Catholic liturgy would be uniform throughout the world. The "Counter Reformation" stemmed the exodus toward Protestantism and regained large areas for the Catholic Church. Poland returned to Catholicism, as did large parts of Germany, France, and the southern Netherlands.

On the positive side, from 1500 to 1650, Catholic missions reached out to Mexico, South America, Africa, India, China, and Japan. Ignatius Loyola (1491-1556) founded the Society of Jesus (Jesuits) in 1534. Through the Jesuits, the Gospel was taken throughout the world. They brought life to the Church in its missionary role. The Jesuits were preachers, builders, teachers, writers, and college founders. In addition, the Capuchin Order was founded in 1528. Frequent reception of the Eucharist and other sacraments increased, as did Mass attendance. Spirituality and piety in the Church grew.

Thomas More (1478–1535), lord chancellor of England, is an example of the great heroes of faith in the Church even during this troubled time. He put his career and his whole life on the line, refusing to be exploited as the king's tool against his conscience and his guide. In 1534, More was tried by Henry VIII on charges of high treason. After almost a year and a half in the tower of London, he was beheaded on July 6, 1535. His last words were "I die as the king's good servant, but as God's servant first." Other inspirational leaders in the Church were Francis of Sales, Charles Borromeo, Theresa of Avila and Joan of Arc, who was martyred in Reims in 1429.

The fifteenth and sixteenth centuries were a period of cultural renaissance. There was a rebirth of interest in classic Greek and Roman culture. Popes patronized the arts in this period. Michelangelo painted the Sistine Chapel. Thomas a' Kempis wrote his great *Imitation of Christ*. There was a great interest in philosophy and intellectual pursuits. A new philosophy called humanism emphasized the importance of man and the individual. Modern science became the faith of the age. Some of the great scientists of this time were Copernicus (1473-1543), Galileo (1564-1642), and a little bit later, Newton (1642-1727).

The Seventeenth and Eighteenth Centuries

The seventeenth century, known as the "Age of Reason," was characterized by doctrinal disputes, religious skepticism, social changes, technical advances, secularism, and humanistic philosophy. Man thought he was too smart for God. The Church was confronted by intellectual philosophers such as Descartes, Pascal, Spinoza, Leibnitz, Voltaire, Hume, Rousseau, and Kant. Denial of any supernatural religion was widespread. Man's primary concern was with this life, not the next. The mind of man, rather than faith, was felt to be the best guide to happiness.

Confidence in man and his power flourished. Human knowledge and reason were glorified. Man would define morality based on his own nature, his own values, his wants, and the needs of society. Intellectuals argued that man is no sinner. He is a "reasonable" creature that needs common sense, not grace or mercy. This philosophy, of course, greatly overestimated the goodness of man. Left to his own devices, man can rationalize anything he wants to do. For example, African slavery began in America during this time.

The Age of Reason was an intellectual revolution. It was the birth of secularism. There was an almost militant attitude toward the faith, especially in France. Many people questioned the truth and relevance of the Bible. People didn't feel bound by old religious traditions and rules anymore. If the intellectuals had any religion, it was deism—the belief in a supreme being, but not a personal God that gets involved in the daily events of our lives. Voltaire (1694-1778) was the most influential spokesman for deism and humanism. He was proud and self-sufficient, and he personified the skepticism of the French enlightenment. During the Age of Reason, man made a deliberate attempt to organize a religiously neutral civilization. Faith had to be confined to the home and hearth. Sounds a bit like our current secular society, doesn't it?

The French Revolution in 1789 posed another threat to the Catholic Church because the Church was considered part of the old order. The French government allowed for the Church but sought to control it by providing for election of bishops and priests like any other civil servants. The pope refused to go along with this. A split resulted between the so-called constitutional (state-recognized) and the nonconstitutional (loyal to Rome) churches. When Austrian and Prussian troops invaded France to put down the revolution, a savage "reign of terror" ensued, and persecution against the nonconstitutional Church intensified. Some 30,000 to 40,000 priests were driven into hiding or exile. Later, the death penalty was imposed on those deportees who dared to return. Eventually, the constitutional Church lost favor as well, and the government sought to "deChristianize" France altogether.

A new calendar was developed deleting Christian references and emphasizing a "cult of reason" and reverence for "idealized nature." Cathedrals were turned into "temples of reason." The new French religion was a philanthropic deism. By 1794 deChristianization had pretty much spent its force and with a decree issued February 21, 1795, free exercise of any religion was guaranteed. There was a rush to reopen the churches.

But just when it seemed that the Catholic Church was at the point of revival in France, Napoleon seized the papal states. The pope excommunicated him. Napoleon proceeded to have the pope arrested and carried off to France in 1808. For nearly six years the pope had to endure a humiliating captivity.

Finally, the Congress of Vienna (1814-1815) brought a general peace to Europe; a peace that lasted a hundred years. It disavowed the revolution and restored the old order. With the downfall of Napoleon came a spiritual and intellectual revival of the Catholic Church. Once more, the Church was a vital institution and a powerful force in public affairs. The revolutionary periods had seen the Church stripped of its privileges, its pope imprisoned, its property confiscated, its monasteries emptied, its priests and nuns slaughtered and driven into exile, its very existence called into question. No wonder the Church became defensive. But after Waterloo, the Church returned to health and vigor. On the cultural side, composers Handel, Mozart, and Hayden all lived during this time.

The seventeenth and eighteenth centuries also marked a struggle by the Church with critical rationalism, Jansenism, and Gallicanism. Jansenism stressed belief in the radical corruption of human nature. It was a pessimistic theology characterized by moral rigorism. According to Jansenism, even man's pretended virtues were vices, and grace was only given to the predestined. Those who weren't predestined to receive grace were doomed to eternal punishment. Gallicanism opposed papal centralization and wanted to restrict papal authority. At the same time, secular governments were encroaching on Church authority.

The Church was now confronted with the question of how it was going to deal with liberalism, a new political movement that espoused the ideas of the enlightenment and the French Revolution. The pioneer of liberal Catholicism was a French priest, Felicitee DeLamennias. Rather than fleeing from liberalism, he wanted to Catholicize it. He espoused complete democracy. He felt that separation of Church and State was important; but he was ahead of his time and the Church rejected him. The pope spoke out against radicalism, naturalism, totalitarianism, materialistic capitalism, and progressive liberalism in the famous "Syllabus of Errors."

Eventually, however, the Church's position on liberalism began to change. Pope Leo XIII saw the importance of the Catholic Church meeting the needs of the age and breaking out of the defensive mentality toward liberalism. Concern over the causes of poverty and awareness of oppressive social structures that perpetuated exploitation and economic inequities in the workplace, etc. led the Church toward a "Social Catholicism." The Church began to address the *causes* of poverty rather than just dealing with problems. It was this social Catholicism that Pope Leo XIII presented in his encyclical "Rerum Novarum," which he issued in 1891. It challenged Catholics to get involved in the struggle for social justice and reform of the social order.

Catholics in the thirteen original colonies in America came here for the same reason as the Puritans and Quakers—to escape persecution. With the political predominance of Protestants in the colonies, however, Catholics were often subjected to severe restrictions on their religious liberty. The American Revolution brought about a change in the fortunes of American Catholics. The legal disabilities under which they labored were gradually lifted, beginning with the adoption of religious liberty in Maryland and Pennsylvania in 1776.

John Carroll of Maryland was the first American bishop. His little flock, which, at his consecration in 1790, numbered 35,000 (out of 4,000,000 Americans), grew to nearly 200,000 by his death in 1815. His diocese was subdivided in 1808 when four other dioceses were added: Boston, Philadelphia, New York, and Bardstown (later Louisville). While thoroughly loyal to Rome, John Carroll was also thoroughly American and committed to the basic principle of separation of Church and State. American Catholics remained consistently in the liberal Catholic camp in this sense at least.

The Church responded to the "Age of Reason" by reemphasizing traditional values. New religious orders were formed and old ones were revived, to teach, evangelize, and care for the sick. Missions expanded worldwide to include Africa, Asia, and the newly discovered lands of North and South America. Some areas, however, such as Japan, feared that foreign missionaries meant foreign invaders. Between 1614 and 1642, more than 4,000 martyrs in such areas made the ultimate witness for Christ–some by sword, some by the stake, some by boiling cauldrons. At the same time, however, the Church's reaction to the Age of Reason was defensive and negative. The Church retreated somewhat from intellectualism. Catholics were not supposed to question or doubt. Certain books were off limits. On the other hand, the Church had its own intellectuals such as John Locke, a Christian philosopher. His teaching was that Christianity has only one essential doctrine–Jesus is the Messiah. Locke also emphasized the importance of a good and moral life.

The Nineteenth Century

The Church, which had been aligned with the aristocracy in Europe, became the church of the common man. Its wealth and power declined drastically. Its emphasis and identification was now with the poor and downtrodden. In some areas of Europe, the Church was "secularized," which was merely a nice word for having its property forcibly taken away and given to the State. Concordats, which specified the terms and conditions under which governments would permit the Church to function, were signed in France (1801), Italy (1803), Bavaria and Sardinia (1817), Russia and Naples (1818), the Netherlands (1827), Switzerland (1828), Spain (1851), and Austria (1855).

From the middle of the nineteenth century on, the Church faced increasing challenges of agnosticism, atheism, materialism, indifference, liberalism, and communism. In describing liberalism, H. Richard Niebuhr stated, "A God without wrath brought men without sin into a kingdom without judgment through the ministrations of a Christ without a cross." The modernistic liberals hoped to be considered serious Christians, but they leaned upon modern thought for their support. Liberal theology reduced distinctions between revelation and natural religion, between Christianity and other religions, between saved and lost, between Christ and other men, and between man and God. In contrast to the biblical view of creation, Charles Darwin came up with his theory of Evolution and wrote *The Origin of Species* in 1859.

A new method of Bible study arose called "higher criticism." This method was not really interested in the literal accuracy of the Bible but instead sought to read between the lines and find out who wrote it, when it was written, and to whom and why it was written. In essence, higher criticism applied the same literary criticism to the Bible as to any other literary work. Some theories of the "higher critics" have been disproved by the Dead Sea Scrolls. In contrast to "higher critics," traditionalists believe the Bible is the true, divinely inspired word of God so it really doesn't matter who wrote it or when, etc.

Liberal theology appeared in New England churches under the title "New Theology." The Congregational church was probably the leader in this movement. Another challenge to the Church at this time was the beginning of new sects such as the Mormons (1830), Jehovah's Witnesses (1872), and Christian Scientists (1876), whose doctrines differ significantly from those of traditional Christianity.

The nineteenth century also saw a significant amount of anti-Catholic sentiment in the U.S. There were defamatory books and pamphlets about the Church, nuns, and priests. The Reverend Lyman Beecher stirred up a mob that proceeded to burn down a convent and a school conducted by Ursuline nuns at Charlestown, Massachusetts. "No papary" gangs burned some churches and lynched a number of Catholics. The Ku Klux Klan reflected the anti-Catholic sentiment in the U.S. There were anti-Catholic riots in Philadelphia (the City of Brotherly Love) in 1844. In 1887, the American Protective Association was organized. Its members swore to never vote for a Catholic and never hire one or go on strike with one if at all possible.

To survive in such hostile surroundings, the American Catholic Church provided an alternative to the Protestant-dominated culture. It developed its own schools, orphanages, hospitals, old-age homes, and other institutions. The Catholic University of America opened in 1889 and quickly became the stronghold of the progressives. The Church developed a strict, uniform theology to confront the various theological and philosophical challenges. The often-misunderstood doctrine of papal infallibility (in matters of faith and morals) appeared in 1870 as a sort of papal sovereignty. It was, at this particular time, an essential prerequisite to an effective papacy. Again, there had to be one chief executive officer of the Church whose word would be law. That chief executive officer was the pope. In Matthew 16:19 Jesus delegates to Peter (and by inference, to the Church) the power of binding and loosing (forbidding and permitting). Whatever Peter forbids or permits on earth will be treated the same way in heaven. To me it was Jesus' way of saying, "Peter, after I return to heaven, what you say goes." The pope, as successor to Peter, has that authority.

The spiritual revival of the Catholic Church during the nineteenth century found an important outlet in missionary zeal. India, China, Japan, Korea, Indonesia, Pakistan, Taiwan, Hong Kong, Ceylon, Malaysia, Burma, Thailand, Vietnam, and Africa were all evangelized by missionaries; but no missionary territory in the nineteenth century registered more sensational gains than the Catholic Church in the U.S. Thanks to the massive influx of Catholic immigrants—Irish, Germans, Italians, Poles, and others—the growth of the Catholic Church far outstripped the nation's growth. By 1850, Roman Catholicism, which was almost invisible at the birth of the nation in terms of numbers, had become the country's largest religious denomination. By 1890, Catholics numbered 8,909,000 out of the total U.S. population of 62,947,000.

The trend toward social Catholicism continued. In the mid-1880s, progressive Catholics began to take more of an interest in such questions as trade unionism and justice for the poor. Gradually, a number of leaders came forward to emphasize the Church's responsibility in bringing about social reform. The National Catholic Welfare Conference was a peacetime coordinating agency for Catholic affairs. The Conference called for legislation to guarantee the right of workers to bargain collectively, a minimum wage act, social security, and health and unemployment insurance. Although denounced as socialistic, all but one of their proposals were later incorporated into the New Deal legislation of the thirties.

The Twentieth Century

One would think that by the twentieth century, mankind would have learned from mistakes of the past and become more enlightened, more peaceful, and more compassionate. Nothing could be further from the truth. There are those who believe mankind is evolving to a higher level of consciousness, but the events of the twentieth century would seriously discredit that theory. As indicated in the beginning of this chapter, some of the most horrible atrocities in the history of the world occurred in the twentieth century.

The Church in the twentieth century had to contend with dictators the likes of Hitler and Mussolini. Pope Pius XI issued the encyclical "Mit Brennender Sorge," which was the first great official public document to confront and criticize Nazism and one of the greatest such condemnations ever issued by the Vatican. Smuggled into Germany, it was read from all the Catholic pulpits on Palm Sunday in March 1937. The Church lent support to persecuted Jews. Pinchas Lapide, former Israeli consul in Italy, credits the Vatican and the Church with saving some 400,000 Jews from certain death. In the occupied areas of eastern Europe, priests and pastors, along with devout laymen, were treated as common criminals. Thousands were executed or sent to concentration camps. Only the demands of the war and the need for popular support prevented the Nazis from eradicating religion from Germany altogether.

At the same time, the Church was faced with the upsurge of antireligious communism. The Communist Revolution in Russia had many of the same traits as Hitler's Germany: dictatorial leadership, a single centralized party, ruthless terror, propaganda, censorship, a controlled economy, and hostility to all organized religion. Lenin believed in violence as the chief vehicle of Marxism. When Lenin died in 1924, a bitter struggle for Soviet leadership raged between Trotsky and Stalin. By 1927, Stalin was the unrivaled dictator. Stalin proved, if anything, even more ruthless than Hitler. He used secret police terror and labor camps to suppress even the slightest dissent and to eliminate all potential rivals.

The Communist Revolution confronted Christianity with an enormous challenge because it was a worldview based on atheism. Thousands of clergymen were imprisoned or "liquidated" during the collectivization of agriculture and Stalin's "purges." "Servants of Religion" continued to be treated as second-class citizens. They were constantly harassed by the secret police as "clerical-fascists." By 1939, the atheistic propaganda, rigid anti-religion laws, and Stalinist terror brought the Russian Orthodox Church to the brink of disintegration. The Lutherans were almost wiped out, and Baptists and evangelical Christian denominations were ravaged.

In 1937, Pope Pius XI issued the encyclical "Divini Redemptoris" condemning the errors of communism. Coming only four days after his encyclical criticizing Nazi Germany, this placed the Vatican firmly on the side of persecuted believers in the totalitarian countries. These encyclicals protested the opposition of the Church and called upon Catholics to resist the idolatrous cults of race and state, to stand against the perversion of Christian doctrines and morality, and to maintain their loyalty to Christ, His church, and Rome.

Another challenge to the Church in the twentieth century was the growth of secularism, which speaks of a world disinterested in God. Secularism doesn't seek to know or do God's will, and it recognizes no standards or values other than those supporting democracy or Marxism. This condition is now so prevalent in Europe that people speak of the "post-Christian era." Many of the same forces are at work in the United States. Court cases have outlawed religious symbols such as Christmas manger scenes on public property, the closing of public offices on Good Friday, and practically any mention of God, the Bible, or religion in public schools.

Prominent Catholic scholar Jean Danielou, warning against the secularization of Christianity itself, says,

> The danger of Christianity at present is that it should become secularized, worldly, reduced to a kind of socialist humanism. This is not what the world needs; and, if Christians were reduced to offering the world only this humanism, they would soon be set aside and rightly so, since there have always been socialist teachers of morality and organizers of society: they have rendered service, but they have never saved anyone. The world today does not need greater social organization but a Savior: man today needs someone who will answer the fundamental problems of his existence, which no social structure has ever been able to answer."[5]

The Catholic Church of the twentieth century continued its emphasis on peace and social justice. The Catholic Interracial Council worked against racial prejudice. Controversial priests and religious have challenged the establishment and undergone persecution and imprisonment for their nonviolent demonstrations against social evils. Many nuns and priests in Latin America were imprisoned, tortured, lynched, and otherwise executed for their opposition to oppressive dictatorships.

In the U.S., Anti-Catholic feeling was still strong enough in the 1920s to enable the Church's enemies to pass immigration restriction laws. By the 1950s, however, it was quite obvious to most observers that the Catholic Church in the U.S. had become a thoroughly American institution. The political significance of this fact was understood when John F. Kennedy was elected the first Catholic president of the United States, an event that, coupled with the reign of Pope John XXIII and the calling of the Second Vatican Council, definitely marked the beginning of a new era in the history of American Catholicism.

We were blessed with sincere, dedicated, and extremely influential popes in the twentieth century. Perhaps the most influential, at least in terms of how he affected the Catholic Church, was our beloved John XXIII. He was a totally new kind of pope: a simple, spontaneous person

[5]Bruce L. Shelley. *Church History in Plain Language.* Waco, TX: Word Books, 1982, pp. 487-488.

who loved life and loved people and was not afraid to show it. Heedless of papal etiquette, he invited friends to his dinner table and wandered through the streets of Rome, speaking with all, visiting hospitals and prisons, making little gestures and telling jokes that soon were repeated around the world. Though John's pontificate was short (only four years and seven months), it resulted in a dramatic revolution in the Church. John emphasized the need for unity of the Body of Christ and extended friendly arms to Christians of other denominations. The Second Vatican Council (1962-1965) brought about tremendous change, reform, and modernization in the Church. It was like a "reformation" within the Church itself.

The Second Vatican Council was, in my opinion, the most important religious event of the twentieth century. It brought some 2500 of the top leaders of the world's largest religious body together for four three-month sessions over four years and engaged them in debate on most of the vital religious issues facing mankind. It issued sixteen documents (four constitutions, nine decrees, and three declarations), which when implemented would produce far-reaching changes in Catholic communities around the world. It was the first ecumenical council in history to assemble with hardly any interference from secular governments, and the first to have other Christians in attendance as official delegates of their respective churches. There were 230 participants from the U.S., second only to Italy, which had 430. There were 230 Africans and 300 from Asia.

The decree on liturgy provided for translating Latin into the modern languages and urged all concerned to make the liturgy intelligible to laymen and to secure their participation in the fullest manner. There was a change from the view of the Church as a hierarchal pyramid structure to the Church as the whole people of God, dwelling on the common priesthood of the faithful. There was also a change in the attitude and practice toward other Christians.

The document on ecumenism put the whole matter of Protestant-Catholic relations in a different perspective. The ultimate goal of ecumenism was not viewed as the return of Protestants to the Catholic Church but rather the reunion of all the separated brethren while recognizing other Christian denominations as true ecclesial communities. Catholics were encouraged to enter into dialogue with other Christians, to engage in common prayer with them, and to work with them on social problems such as abortion, racism, and economic injustice. Emphasis was placed on the basic elements of the Christian tradition that were already held in common with other Christians.

All in all, the Second Vatican Council was a giant step back toward the original spiritual foundations of the early Church. A tidal wave of change was set in motion by Vatican II. In the liturgy, the altar was suddenly brought forward. The priest now faced the congregation. Instead of whispering prayers in Latin, he now said them aloud in the language of the people. Previously, the faithful were expected to maintain a quiet and private reverence. Now, we were told to turn and greet those around us with a sign of peace. The emphasis was on community worship rather than private worship.

For many of us who were raised in the old Church, the changes were comparable to the tearing down of the Berlin Wall. Most welcomed the changes, but some were threatened and bewildered by them. In addition to changes in the Mass, there were changes in the way we celebrate the sacraments. Communal penance, as opposed to private confession, was one example. Last rites (extreme unction) is now called the sacrament of the sick, and it isn't reserved for those who are on their deathbeds.

Along with the new freedoms came controversy. Whereas we previously had apparent uniformity, we now had different Catholics with different opinions. The Vatican II Church is more democratic than ever before. Individual Catholics have a greater awareness of their own personal responsibility. We all have to pray, read the Scriptures, and discern what God wants us to do in given situations. Vatican II forced us to reexamine our traditions in light of sacred Scripture. The process has been somewhat disruptive, but very beneficial overall.

On June 3, 1963, just before the opening of the second session of the Council, John XXIII died. Pope Paul VI, however, took over where John left off and continued with the work. The innovations created some inevitable divisions among Catholics. Some clergy remained conservative and attempted to preserve the past. Among the progressives, some chose to emphasize the social message of Christianity. In fact, in Latin American, some cast their lot with a form of Marxism. Other progressives took a more spiritual approach by stressing a return to the Bible and Christian living. Despite all the confusion, we came out of the Second Vatican Council as a stronger, more dynamic and, in my opinion, more Christian Church.

The Twenty-First Century

Today, the Roman Catholic Church is the largest denomination in the United States. It is a Church on the move. It is vibrant, alive, and reaching out to all people. It is actively involved in spreading God's word, giving spiritual direction, and speaking out forcefully on social and moral issues such as abortion, poverty, peace, social justice, and spiritual renewal. It is a Church that serves with works of charity, missionary activities, and educational activities. It is a Church that emphasizes the Word of God, sharing faith in Jesus Christ and evangelizing the world. It is a Church that strives to practice what it preaches; a Church that puts its money where its mouth is.

The Church of today tends to be a Church of committed Catholics. We tend to be Catholic by choice nowadays rather than simply because we were born that way. More and more laymen are studying their faith, taking seminary courses, and getting involved in various ministries such as evangelism, lectoring, and visiting the sick. Laymen are also more involved in Church administration.

We are a Church that realizes there is room under our roof for differing viewpoints of Scripture and theology. Traditional Catholics emphasize the sacraments and the sacredness of our liturgy. Evangelical Catholics emphasize the importance of Scripture, Bible study, and evangelization. Charismatic Catholics emphasize the gifts and power of the Holy Spirit. Liberal Catholics remind us of the openness to change and the growth we must have in order to be relevant and effective in our modern world. Conservative Catholics emphasize the importance of maintaining our historical traditions and institutions. We complement each other, help each other, and need each other to function as a Christian community.

The voices for change that came with Vatican II continue to be heard. Issues such as divorce, birth control, clergy celibacy, and the role of women in the Church are vigorously debated in the Church today. Modern theologians often disagree with each other, and yet all consider themselves Roman Catholics. One of the most promising signs of renewal in the Church was the growth of the Charismatic or Neo-Pentecostal movement (see Chapter 9).

With the expansion of democracy and the decline of communism throughout the world, the future promises to be very interesting with regard to how Christianity and Catholicism fare in the face of increased freedom. Despite all the renewal and revival in the Church, however, our world continues to be plagued by war, poverty, crime, divorce, racism, violence, sexual perversion, alcoholism, drugs, and widespread decline in church attendance. The Catholic Church has not and must not cave in to pressures to lower its standards of morality. We may not always like what the Bible says, but we cannot change it to fit our lifestyle. We may not always agree with the pope, but he is our "chief executive officer," and we have to listen to what he says.

What does the Church have going for it as it heads into the challenges of the future? It has a unique history that dates back to the origin of Christianity. It has members from virtually every culture and geographical area. It has a strong bond of tradition and unity. It has a strong sacramental base that strengthens it and builds it up as a community of believers. It has an intangible Catholic wisdom derived from great philosophers, theologians, and saints through the ages. It has a sensitivity and tolerance for the frailty of mankind while still maintaining an uncompromised commitment to the lofty ideals of the Gospel.

I would like to give credit to the book "A Concise History of the Catholic Church" by Thomas Bokenkotter (listed in Bibliography), which I used extensively as a reference for the information contained in this chapter. It is a very well researched and scholarly work on the subject and I highly recommend it to those desiring a more comprehensive and detailed account of Church history.

CHAPTER IV

The Catholic Bible

Extra Books?

Why does the Catholic Bible have more books than Protestant Bibles? Some people seem to think that the Catholic Church added some extra books to the Bible. Actually, the opposite is true. We didn't add them; the Protestants (beginning with the Puritans) deleted them. The so-called Apocryphal or Deuterocanonical books were included in the Septuagint, the Greek Bible in use in Jesus' time. They were in the Latin Vulgate, which was the earliest complete Bible with both Old and New Testaments. They were in Luther's German translation of 1534. They were in Cloverdale's English Bible of 1535. They were in the King James Version of 1611. In fact, they had a place in all English translations of the Bible in the sixteenth century.

The original controversy over these books was between St. Jerome and St. Augustine. St. Jerome was a great biblical scholar. His translation of the Bible (the Vulgate) was excellent for its day. But Jerome did have his idiosyncrasies. He felt that any Old Testament books that were not found in the Hebrew language should not be included in the canon of Scripture. In contrast, St. Augustine, a great theologian and a contemporary of Jerome, felt that all of these books should be included in the canon of Scripture. Finally, a compromise was reached, and these books were included as a separate section of the Bible. They remained that way up until the Protestant Reformation. After the Reformation, the Protestants eventually removed them altogether and the Catholics included them in the Old Testament.

The following is a discussion of the history of the Bible and an overview of the Deuterocanonical books.

The Septuagint: The Old Testament was translated into Greek even before there was a New Testament. In the centuries immediately preceding the Christian era, the Jews became widely scattered. A large colony of Jews was located in Alexandria, Egypt, and their native tongue, Hebrew, was hardly used, being superseded by the Greek. In order that the Hebrew Scriptures not be lost, a group of 70 (or 72) scholars was commissioned by the high priest in Jerusalem to make a translation into Greek. This was in about the middle of the third century B.C. The name of this translation, "Septuagint," comes from the Latin word for seventy and is commonly abbreviated by using the Roman numeral LXX.

The LXX received the endorsement of eminent rabbis and within a short time was being widely used by the Jews and their Gentile proselytes in the Greek-speaking world. It was only natural that the LXX became the Old Testament that was read in the early Christian churches. The authors of the New Testament books used the LXX when they quoted the Old Testament. Many copies of the LXX, dating from the third century A.D., have been of great help to scholars in determining the original Hebrew text.

The Vulgate: Latin, the official language of the Roman Empire, gradually replaced Greek in the Roman Church and became the language of the liturgy of the Church. Various versions of the Scriptures in what is known as Old Latin came into use. Finally, with the approval and aid of Pope Damascus, St. Jerome (340-420 A.D.) undertook the translation of the Bible to Latin. He went to Bethlehem, where he could visit the places mentioned in the Bible, and there completed the translation of the Scriptures known as the Vulgate. This Latin translation became the official Bible of the Roman Catholic Church. The first book printed in moveable type, the Gutenberg Bible, was Jerome's Latin Vulgate.

The Douai Bible: Until this Bible was published, the only Bible used by the Roman Catholic Church was the Vulgate, the Latin version of the Scriptures based on the work of Jerome. With Gutenberg's invention of moveable type, books could be produced in larger number and at much less expense than could the old handwritten Bibles. Several unauthorized translations of the Catholic Bible were produced in native languages. Bible scholars wanted a more accurate translation in the English language. This led the Roman Catholic authorities to approve an English version. The work on the Catholic version was done at a Roman Catholic college in Douai, Flanders. Chief among the English translators was Gregory Martin, formerly a fellow of St. John's College at Oxford. During this time the college moved to Rheims, where the New Testament was produced in 1582, and then back to Douai.

Because of financial troubles, the Old Testament was not published until 1609.

This translation, known as the Douai version or the Rheims-Douai Bible, became the official Roman Catholic Bible in English. Until recent times, this was the only English translation receiving the official sanction of the Roman Catholic Church.

What Are You Missing?

Unfortunately, most Bibles today do not include the Apocryphal or Deuterocanonical Books. What are you missing if your Bible does not include them? The following book-by- book sketch will give you a little idea.

Tobit

Tobit is a fascinating story of romance and faith, replete with excellent and practical moral teaching. It was written around the second century B.C. Chapter 4 of this book is a beautiful account of a dying father's advice to his son. It warns against such things as pride and waste (4:4) and excessive drinking (4:15). It encourages us to bless the Lord and ask for his guidance (4:19). It provides guidance on such things as giving (4:7-11, 16–17) and an employer's duty to pay his employees promptly (4:14). It states the Golden Rule (4:15). Later, in chapter 10, verse 13, advice is given to a young bride.

The book deals with such current, up-to-date problems as a wife having to support the family while her husband suffers the stress and humiliation of unemployment and disability. It illustrates the frustration and strain on a marriage that can result from these circumstances (2:11-14). It deals with money problems (5:19) and the problem of parents worrying about their son (chapter 10). It also deals with spiritual concepts such as tithing (1:7), prophecy fulfilled (2:6), God's promise of prosperity and blessings to those who are faithful to him, God bringing man and woman together for marriage, healing, and a beautiful prayer of repentance (3:1-8). It mentions the feast of Pentecost (the feast of weeks; 2:1).

This book actually gives added credence to the Book of Jonah. Like Jonah, it takes place in Nineveh (1:10). Tobias is taken captive by the Assyrians. A fish tries to swallow Tobias, but unlike with Jonah, the fish does not succeed (6:3).

The book also deals with angels and the concept of a guardian angel. There are only three angels specifically named in the Bible, and one of them (Raphael) is mentioned in this book. He is one of the seven angels who stand before the Lord (12:15). The only other angels specifically mentioned in the Bible are Michael and Gabriel.

Rather than quoting the actual verses, I will let you read the book for yourself. I think you will find it interesting, enjoyable, and edifying.

Judith

This book is a great testimony of faith and courage. Judith was a descendent of another Bible hero, Gideon. She was a widow. Her husband was overseeing gleaners when he died of heat stroke. Judith was wealthy and beautiful, but after her husband's death, she wore sackcloth and fasted. She had been a widow three years and four months. Chapter 8 verse 8 says, "She was greatly renowned among all, because she feared the Lord very much, neither was there any one who spoke an ill word of her."

Chapter 5 of the book is a concise history lesson on the Jewish people, including the time before, during and after the Exodus. It is a good lesson for us as well. No one could triumph over Israel except when the people departed from the worship of the Lord their God (5:17-18).

During the reign of Nebuchadnezzar, he sends his general, Holofernes, against all the kingdoms that resisted him. General Holofernes is quite successful until he comes up against Israel. When Holofernes comes against Israel, the people of Israel hold an all-night prayer session (6:21). Holofernes cuts off their water supply (chapter 7). The Israelites turn against their king, Uzziah, just as they had turned against Moses in the desert. Uzziah sets a waiting period of five days, sort of like putting a fleece before the Lord. If the Lord doesn't rescue them within five days, they will give in.

When Judith hears of Uzziah's promise to surrender after five days, she calls the elders and gives them a good scolding. Her advice to them is good advice to all of us about "putting the Lord to the test." She says,

Who are you to tempt the Lord? This is not a promise that may draw down mercy, but rather that may stir up wrath, and enkindle indignation. You have set a limit to the mercy of the Lord, and you have told him to act as it pleases you. (8:11-13)

She continues to chastise the elders, telling them that the very lives of the people depend on the elders, and here they are, going along with the people. The elders should be reminding people of the trials their fathers faced and how they overcame them. They should comfort the people's hearts by their speech and encourage their faith. That is what ministers are supposed to do. She encourages the elders to humble themselves before God and be patient. She reminds them that God isn't like a man. He can't be threatened.

Uzziah and the elders are convicted by her words and respond, "All that you have said is true and no one can deny your words. So now pray for us, for you are a holy woman who fears God." Judith comes up with a plan but asks that it be kept secret. She asks Uzziah and the elders not to ask her what the plan is, but just to trust that it is of God and to pray for her. Chapter 9 is Judith's beautiful intercessory prayer for victory over the godless enemy.

In chapter 10, Judith gets all dressed up, making herself as beautiful as possible. She goes toward the Assyrian camp until they apprehend her. She tells them she is a Hebrew but she knows the Israelites won't surrender and they will be conquered so she wants to join the Assyrians as a spy. She says she wants to tell Holofernes all the Israelites' secrets so they can take the Hebrews without losing a single man. She really butters the general up and tells him that God will punish the Hebrews through him. Holofernes likes what he hears and falls for it hook, line, and sinker.

Holofernes is tempted by Judith's beauty. He gets drunk and falls asleep. Then this sweet, holy woman chops off his head. She puts his head in her food bag and goes back to the Hebrew fortress. She tells the Israelites to go out like they are going to attack in the morning. The Assyrians will run to the leader, and when they find him dead and wallowing in his own blood, they will panic and flee. "Then you can go after them and the Lord will destroy them." And that is exactly what happens. The book ends with something that sounds like a charismatic prayer meeting, with music, singing, and praising the Lord (chapter 16).

For those people who feel the Bible does not give much credit to women, it is unfortunate that this book is not included in their Bible. Judith is a real heroine, and her advice to spiritual and temporal leaders is excellent.

Baruch

Baruch was written during the Babylonian captivity after the Chaldeans had captured Jerusalem and destroyed it by fire. Chapters 1 and 2 deal with repentance for the sins that led to their captivity. These sins actually included men eating the flesh of their own sons and daughters (chapter 2:3)! Of course, our society is much more civilized than that. We don't eat our sons and daughters, we just abort them—by the millions. Incredibly, our law protects those who commit abortions and prosecutes those who try to prevent them. Are we really that much more civilized?

In chapter 2, verses 30 through 32 recall a prophecy given to Moses:

> In their exile they will remember these words and they will realize that I am the Lord their God. I shall give them an understanding heart and an attentive ear. Then they will praise me in the land of their captivity and will recall my name.

Sometimes God has to allow people to hit rock bottom before they remember Him and turn back to Him.

Chapter 3 is again a prayer of repentance and forgiveness. Israel lost its wisdom and knowledge because it lost the source of wisdom and knowledge (God) and looked elsewhere. He who created the wondrous works of nature, He alone has wisdom; and He offered a share of it to Jacob and Israel.

In chapter 4, God calls His people back to his word and his law. There is hope! God did not turn His people over to their enemies for destruction—only for chastisement; to bring them back, to teach them. There is comfort: "He will deliver you from the trap of your enemies."

God may allow us to suffer at times, but He will never leave us or forsake us. He will deliver us and bring us back. Sometimes we may get away from God through sin. We may backslide. He may have to chastise us and allow us to suffer calamity to bring us to our knees again. This is not a popular message in our "positive confession" society, but it is scriptural. Maybe one reason for the false doctrine that if you are Christian nothing bad will happen to you—the "heaven on earth" philosophy, the "name it and claim it, God wants you rich" philosophy—is the absence of this book from non-Catholic Bibles.

Chapter 6 describes the false gods of Babylon and tells the people not to fear them, and to not give in to idolatry. The images are powerless and worthless. How can mortal men be gods?

Wisdom

This book personifies wisdom and extols her virtues. It is speaking, of course, of divine wisdom, not human wisdom. I believe that when the Bible speaks of wisdom as a person, it is referring to the third person of the Trinity, the Holy Spirit. In chapter 1, verses 7 through 9 tell us that the Spirit of God holds all things together, knows all things, knows our thoughts, knows our words, and convicts us of our sins. Chapter 9, verse 17 actually mentions the Holy Spirit: "And who will know your thoughts, except you give wisdom, and send your Holy Spirit from above?"

This book contains excellent teachings on several topics. If you want to read a beautiful, poetic, and logical treatise on the futility and foolishness of idolatry, read chapter 13. If you want a response to materialism, verses 8 through 12 of chapter 5 say,

> What has pride profited us? All those things have passed away like a shadow, and like a rumor that slips away. As a ship passes through the waves, which when it has gone, no trace can be found, nor the track of its keel in the waters; or as when a bird flies through the air, no track of its passage can be found, but only the sound of wings beating the light air and parting it by the force of its flight; it moved its wings and passed through, and there is no mark found afterwards of its path. Or as when an arrow is shot at a target, the divided air presently comes together again, so that no one knows its route.

Chapter 3 verse 11 tells us that those who reject divine wisdom are unhappy and unfruitful, and their children are spoiled. We need only look at our own humanistic society to see how true that statement is.

Chapter 5 gives us a beautiful Old Testament reference to eternal life. Verse 14 tells us that sinners will speak with regret of their sins in hell; but verse 16 says the just will live forevermore. They will receive a kingdom of glory and a crown of beauty at the hand of the Lord (5:17). Verses 18 through 24 provide an Old Testament parallel to the "armor of God" in Ephesians chapter 6.

One of my favorite teachings in the Book of Wisdom concerns the difficult subject of death. Without a doubt, one of the most painful ordeals a person can suffer is the death of a loved one. This is especially true if the lost loved one is a child or a spouse. When these things happen, we are sometimes inclined to blame God. If God is so good and loving, how can such tragedies be part of his plan for us?

The answer given in this book is that they are not part of his plan. Death was never God's plan for humanity. He didn't invent death and He takes no pleasure in the destruction of the living (1:13). God created humankind to be imperishable, immortal, in his own image and nature. He intended that we would live in perfect harmony with nature, with God, and with each other. It was through the envy of the devil that death came into the world (2:23-25). By sinning and choosing evil over good, we in effect chose Satan over God. That gave Satan some power and authority in the world. I believe that is why nature is somewhat out of balance; why we have killer storms, earthquakes, and other natural disasters; why some of the animals are rebellious and dangerous to man; etc. It seems to me that the more sin and evil there is in the world, the more of these tragedies and disasters we see. The consequences of evil are indiscriminate. They affect us all. It is my belief that that is why bad things sometimes happen to good people. It isn't God's plan, will, or desire. He doesn't rejoice in these things. The good news is that no matter what happens to us, God can make all things work together for good as long as we continue to love Him and praise Him (Romans 8:28).

Much of the Book of Wisdom has prophetic overtones relating to Jesus. Chapter 2, verses 13, 16, and 18–20, for example, describe how the people would conspire against Jesus:

He boasts that he has the knowledge of God, and calls himself the son of God . . . and rejoices that he has God for his Father . . . . If he is the true son of God, God will defend him and will deliver him from the hands of his enemies. Let us test him by indignities and tortures, that we may know his meekness and try his patience. Let us condemn him to a most shameful death, for, according to him, God will protect him.

Chapters 5 and 6 describe the second coming of Christ and how some people will react to it:

He will stand with great constancy against those who have afflicted him. Those who see him will be troubled with a terrible fear, and will be amazed at the suddenness of his unexpected salvation. They will speak to each other in repentance and groaning, in anguish of spirit saying: "This is the man we once held in derision and as an example of reproach. We fools thought his life was madness and his end without honor."(5:1-4)

Chapter 6, verse 6 says, "He will come to you terribly and quickly, because severe judgment will occur for those who rule." Chapter 3, verse 8 tells us that the righteous will govern nations in the kingdom and the Lord will reign forever. Again, this could relate to the second coming of Christ, when he will establish his Kingdom here on earth.

Ecclesiasticus (The Book of Sirach)

This book was written in approximately 132 B.C. It was written in Hebrew by a man named Joshua (or Jesus) but later translated by his grandson into Greek. Like Proverbs, it is a book of profound, supernatural wisdom on numerous subjects.

Like the Book of Wisdom, the first part of the book praises a personified divine wisdom:

All wisdom comes from the Lord God, and is with him before all time, until eternity. Who has numbered the sands of the sea, the drops of rain and the days of the world? Who has measured the height of heaven, the breadth of the earth and the depth of the abyss? (1:1-2)

These questions point out the ignorance of man's wisdom compared to God's. They are reminiscent of the great questions raised in Job chapter 38. Speaking of this personified wisdom, the author goes on to say, "He created her in the Holy Spirit, and saw her, numbered her and measured her" (1:9).

In this book you will find practical advice about numerous topics, including life's hardships, sickness, death, mourning the dead, relationships, friendships, false friends, government, business, borrowing and lending, wealth, children, duty to parents, child raising, heads of households,, dreams, travel, scholars, workers and wages, values, the wonders of nature, the greatness of God, God's justice, trusting in God, good works, virtue, keeping secrets, hospitality, humility, fear of the Lord, manners, charity to the poor, sincerity, self-control, temperance, moderation, priests, tradition, worship, the law, real happiness, health and healing, doctors, sin, shame, pride, loose talk, lying, swearing, evil speech, sins of the flesh, adultery, hypocrisy, and revenge.

Chapter 36 is a wonderful prayer for Israel and for the heathen nations: "Send your fear upon the nations that have sought after you, that they may know there is no God but you and that they may show forth your wonders. Lift up your hand over the strange nations that they may see your power" (36:2-3). Chapter 39 includes a hymn of praise to the Creator, as does Chapter 42. Chapters 44 to 50 (like Hebrews chapter 11 in the New Testament) comprise an inspired history lesson on great faith heroes like Enoch, Noah, Abraham, Isaac, Jacob, Moses, David, Joshua, Samuel, Nathan, Solomon, Elisha, Isaiah, Josiah, Nehemiah, and Joseph.

With regard to family relationships, Chapter 3 verse 6 contains a promise: "He who honors his father will have joy in his own children, and in the day of his prayer he will be heard." Chapter 3, verses 14 and 15 state,

> Son, support the old age of your father and grieve him not in his life; and, if his understanding fails, have patience with him and despise him not when you are in your maturity, for kindness to a father shall not be forgotten.

The following are some additional words of wisdom on various topics:

Witnessing: "Do not hesitate to speak when salvation is at stake" (4:28).

Salvation: "Do not delay to be converted to the Lord or put it off from day to day" (5:8).

Lending: "If you lend, count it as lost. Do not give surety beyond your means; but if you do give bond, presume you will have to pay it" (8:15-16).

Over-involvement: "My son, do not meddle with many affairs; and if you get over-involved you will suffer for it: hurrying after, you will not overtake; and you will not escape by running away" (11:10).

Mankind: "He created out of him a helpmate like to himself; he gave them counsel, and a tongue, eyes, ears and a mind for thinking; and he filled them with knowledge and understanding. He created in them the knowledge of the spirit; he filled their hearts with wisdom and showed them both good and evil. He set his light in their hearts to show them the greatness of his works that they might praise the name which he has sanctified and glory in his wondrous acts, that they might declare the glories of his works" (17:5-8).

Grief and Worry: "Sadness has killed many and there is no profit in it. Envy and anger shorten a man's days and worry will bring old age before one's time" (30:25-26).

Drinking: "Wine drunk with excess raises quarrels, anger and much grief. Wine drunk to excess is bitterness of the soul. Drunkenness is the stumbling block of the fool, reducing his strength and causing wounds" (31:38-40).

Estate planning: "Do not give to your son or wife, brother or friend power over yourself while you live; and do not give your property to another lest you change and must beg it back" (33:20).

Giving: "Give glory to God with a good heart and do not hold back the first fruits of your labor. In every gift show a cheerful face and sanctify your tithes with joy. Give to the Most High as he has given to you and generously offer what your hands have produced" (35:10-12).

Welfare: "When a man must depend on another's table, he exists but does not live; for he feeds his soul with another man's meat" (40:29).

Liturgy, (Referring to David): "He assigned singers before the altar to make sweet melody. He added beauty to the festivals and set in order the solemn times throughout the year that they should praise the holy name of the Lord and magnify the holiness of God in the morning" (47:11-12).

One aspect of Christianity that has suffered from some bad teaching and confusion is the question of "healing." Some people have even died because so-called "faith healers" told them they didn't need their medicine anymore; they didn't need their doctors. I know that God heals. I have seen him heal others, and I have experienced his healing in my own life. But what exactly is the relationship between divine healing and medicine? This book sets the matter straight:

> Honor the physician for the need you have of him, for the Most High has created him. All healing is from God and he will receive gifts from the king. . . . The Most High has created medicines out of the earth and a wise man will not despise them . . . . By these he will cure and will remove their pains and of these the pharmacist makes healing compounds and will make up ointments for health. . . . My son, do not neglect yourself in sickness but pray to the Lord and he will heal you. Turn away from sin and order your hands aright and cleanse your heart from all sin. . . . Then give the physician his place for the Lord created him. Let him not depart from you for his works are necessary. For there is a time when you must fall into the hands of doctors and they will beseech the Lord that he bless what they prescribe to relieve and cure for your preservation. (38:1-2, 4-5, 7, 9-10, 12-14)

1 Maccabees

This book describes events in Jewish history from about 175 to 134 B.C. from the perspective of a family and their faithful struggle against the enemies of Israel. The title is taken from the first hero introduced by the book, Judas Maccabeus, thought to be taken from the Hebrew Maqqabah, meaning "hammer."

This book includes accounts of corruption, espionage, heroism, betrayal, fierce loyalty, deception, political ambition, violence, war, torture, excitement, adventure, victory, defeat, faithfulness, danger, threats, paganism versus Judaism, and, in the midst of all this, faith, serious prayer, fasting, and weeping to the Lord. In short, it has all the elements of a modern best-seller and more. Again, the theme comes through that times of trouble bring out the strongest faith. As we read it, we can relate it to things that have happened in our own lifetime and things yet to come. The book encourages us to stand fast against the enemy now and in the end times.

In the end times, many will fall away rather than face persecution. In chapter 1, unfaithful Jews are trying to make peace with their enemies, compromising their faith and giving in to pagan practices. The temple is desecrated. There are false promises of peace. Religious practices are forbidden (reminiscent of modern communism and the time of the Antichrist to come).

In chapter 2, Mattathias and his five sons (one of which was Judas, called Maccabeus) would not go along with the pagan practices. They separated themselves and remained faithful. They fought against King Antiochus. They drew other faithful Jews to them and formed an army. As he dies, Mattathias gives his son a beautiful blessing (2:51-64). He reminds his sons to "remember that through all generations all who trust in God are strong" (2:61). He appoints Judas Maccabeus as leader of the army (2:66).

The philosophy of Judas Maccabeus is that "success in battle is not in the number of the army but in the strength that comes from heaven" (3:19). Chapter 3, verses 50 to 54 comprise a prayer of desperation, pleading with God to look at what has been done to His people: "How can we stand unless you help us?" This should be our prayer as well, for it is not by might, not by power, but by His Spirit that we will prevail (Zechariah 4:6).

There are lessons on military strategy in chapter 4. Attack while the enemy is divided. No wonder General George Patton said he read the Bible every day! The Israelites did not worry about life or death (4:35). Perhaps that is why they were such formidable adversaries. We should worry even less about life or death since we have the promise of eternal life.

Chapter 6 talks about peace treaties made and broken. Chapter 8 describes a peace with the Romans, but chapter 12 reveals that every time the Jews trusted their enemies and their peace treaties, they were betrayed. Chapter 10 talks about Alexander and Cleopatra. All the nations around Israel sought to destroy them. Chapter 15 gives the biblical perspective on the Middle East crises:

We have neither taken other men's land, nor other men's goods. What we have is the inheritance of our fathers, which had been unjustly occupied by our enemies. When the chance arose, we reclaimed the inheritance of our fathers. (15:33-34)

To this day, the nation of Israel stands as a fulfillment of the Scripture "If God is for us, who is against us?" (Romans 8:31). We need to trust in God, not in our peace treaties, and not in enemies who pretend to be friends.

2 Maccabees

This book is the continuation of 1 Maccabees. If anything, 2 Maccabees is even more brutal and graphic in its description of the violence of the day than 1 Maccabees.

In Chapter 3, Simon, the temple manager, turns traitor and tells the king how to get at the temple treasury. But through divine intervention, the king's representative, Heliodorus, is converted. He goes back and testifies of the power of God. The temple treasury is saved.

Chapter 4 tells of corruption and backsliding. The Greeks force their lifestyle on the Jews. Jason, the high priest, got his position by bribing the king. Corrupt priests hastened to adopt the pagan lifestyle. There were sacrileges in the temple.

In Chapter 5, Jason turns on his own people. He kills his countrymen without mercy. Young and old were slaughtered—women, children, infants; it didn't make any difference. Judas Maccabeus escapes into the wilderness with companions.

In Chapter 6, the king defiles the temple and renames it "the temple of Jupiter Olympius." But these calamities are viewed by the faithful as correction rather than destruction of the nation (6:13): "For it is a token of great goodness when sinners are not allowed to proceed in their ways for a long time but are immediately punished." Again, the idea is that God sometimes has to allow people to suffer to stop them from backsliding. Eleazar is tortured because he refuses to eat pork.

Chapter 7 tells of the heroic courage of seven brothers and their mother. They are all arrested and tortured with whips and scourges in order to make them violate the law by eating pork. The point is that by eating pork, they would be, in effect, denying their God. Their tongues are cut out, they are scalped, their hands and feet are cut off, and they are fried in a pan. One by one, the brothers are tortured this way in front of their mother. Finally, she too is put to death. Verse 36 gives another Old Testament reference to the belief in eternal life: "For my brothers, having undergone a short pain, will now receive eternal life" (see also 7:9, 14, 23). Those who say that the Old Testament Jews had no concept of an afterlife should read this book.

In chapter 8, Judas Maccabeus recruits an army and begins retaking cities and towns, attacking by surprise. In chapter 9, King Antiochus gets his just deserts. First he is smitten with a terrible illness. Then he is thrown out of his chariot. He is bruised all over. Maggots swarm out of his body. His flesh rots away. The stench of his decay makes his army sick. Thus, this monarch who was formerly puffed up with pride is brought low and humbled. Finally, on his deathbed, he repents and writes a prayerful apology to the Jews (9:19-27).

Brutality toward the Jews continues in chapter 12. The men of Joppa invite Jewish families for a boat ride. When they are a good ways out from shore, they throw the Jewish families in, drowning no less than 200. The concept of praying for the dead is mentioned (12:44-46).

Chapter 14 portrays perhaps the most brutal scene. A Jewish man trapped by the enemy stabs himself, runs through a crowd spurting blood on them, and literally rips his guts out and throws them on the crowd. Chapter 15 recounts a betrayal by the commander Nicanor. Judas retaliates. He cuts off Nicanor's head and arm, carries them to Jerusalem, cuts out Nicanor's tongue and feeds it to the birds, hangs up the hand near the temple, and impales Nicanor's head at the top of the citadel as a sign of the help of God.

All in all, 1 and 2 Maccabees would make a great modern movie. It would probably be a box office smash. Yet, for all the violence in these books, they say a lot about faith and courage in days of trouble. May we all have such faith if we ever have to face such persecution and torture.

Conclusion

Hopefully you now have some idea of what you are missing if your Bible does not include the Deuterocanonical books. These books were in the Bible in the beginning, and in my opinion, it is very unfortunate that they have been removed from most modern Bibles. They should be read, reverenced, studied, and meditated on.

Perhaps an appropriate way to end this chapter is with a blessing from 2 Maccabees 1:2-5:

> May God be good to you and remember the covenant he made with Abraham, Isaac and Jacob, his faithful servants, and give you all a desire to worship him, and to do his will with a loving heart and generous spirit. May he open your mind to his law and to his commandments, and grant you peace. May he hear your prayers, and be reconciled to you, and may he never forsake you in the time of evil.

"Man shall not live by bread alone, but by every word that proceeds from the mouth of God." (Matthew 4:4)

CHAPTER V

The Mass

A "Sacrifice of Praise"
(Hebrews 13:15)

Introduction

I have been to a fair number and variety of Christian churches but, in all honesty, I would have to say that the Catholic Mass is the most complete form of community worship I have found. It includes praise, worship, fellowship, confession, repentance, intercessory prayer, private prayer, community prayer, Scripture, preaching, singing, a profession of faith, a free will offering, silence, meditation, symbolism, and, most importantly, Holy Communion. The Mass is our way of, as Hebrews 12:28 puts it, "offering to God acceptable worship with reverence and awe."

But is it scriptural? Absolutely! Many of the beautiful symbols, rituals, and prayers of the Catholic Mass parallel specific instructions and guidelines God gave for worship in the Old Testament as well as the New Testament. What the Catholic Church has done is taken the Old Testament symbols and rituals and translated them into a New Testament context.

The parts of the Mass are familiar to most Catholics, but it is worthwhile to explain them and discuss their scriptural basis. That will be the focus of this chapter.

Preparation

On our way to Mass and as we wait for Mass to begin, we should try to spend some time in prayer for the priest. Pray that the Lord will inspire him and minister through him. Pray that the priest will preach the message the Lord wants His people to hear. Pray for all the people who will be at the Mass; that they will be touched by the Lord and that He will minister to them in the way that they need to be ministered to. Finally, we should pray for ourselves and ask the Lord to help us worship Him in spirit and in truth (John 4:24). We should ask Him to help us really participate in the Mass and pay attention so it will minister to us and we will get the most out of it. We should thank God for this opportunity to participate in the celebration of the Eucharist.

The priest should also pray before celebrating the Mass. The St. Joseph Missal, pages 632-638, lists several optional prayers, including Psalm 130, which may be said in a back-and-forth manner, with the priest and laity alternating verses. There is also a prayer to the Holy Spirit before Mass, the prayer of St. Ambrose, the prayer of St. Thomas Aquinas, and other prayers. Immediately before Mass, the priest may gather for prayer with the lay ministers who will participate in the Mass with him. Some priests may ask the lay people to pray for him with the laying on of hands for the inspiration of the Holy Spirit.

As we enter the Church before Mass, we should dip our hand in the blessed water used for Baptism and make the Sign of the Cross as a symbol of the renewal of our Baptism, saying: "In the name of the Father, and of the Son, and of the Holy Spirit, amen." That, in itself, is a prayer in preparation for Mass. As we enter the church, we can also greet our friends and fellow Christians and engage in fellowship. At the very beginning of Mass, before the entrance hymn, the choir director or other lay person may invite the congregation to greet those people seated around them with a gesture of friendship.

The Entrance Hymn

Music is a very important part of the Catholic liturgy. Paul tells us in Colossians 3:16 that we should sing psalms and hymns and spiritual songs with thankfulness in our hearts to God. Psalm 100:1-2 tells us, "Make a joyful noise to the Lord, all the lands! Serve the Lord with gladness! Come into his presence with singing!" Psalm 100:4 tells us to "Enter his gates with thanksgiving, and his courts with praise!" This is what we do in the entrance hymn; we enter the presence of the Lord with a joyful song of praise. The entrance hymn usually relates to the theme of the Scripture readings for the day. The purpose of the song is to open the celebration, deepen the unity of the people, introduce us to the theme of the season or feast, and accompany the procession.

The Greeting

Led by the priest, the community makes the Sign of the Cross in the name of the Trinity. The priest then formally greets the assembly with words drawn from Scripture, such as 2 Corinthians 13:14: "The grace of the Lord Jesus Christ and the love of God and the fellowship of the Holy Spirit be with you all." The congregation responds, "And also with you."

Penitential Rite

In order to cleanse our hearts to worship the Lord, we pause to examine our conscience, confess our sins, and repent. We acknowledge that we are sinful at times and that we need the transforming love and mercy that God offers to us through His sacrifice for our salvation. Scripture tells us in Psalm 51:17, "The sacrifice acceptable to God is a broken spirit; a broken and contrite heart, O God, thou wilt not despise." When we come to Mass in a spirit of humility and penance, God can renew our broken spirit and create in us a clean heart (Psalm 51:10).

Gloria

The Gloria is an ancient hymn in which the Church, assembled in the Spirit, praises and prays to the Father and the Lamb. It may be sung by the congregation, the people alternately with the choir, or by the choir alone. There are many beautiful musical arrangements of the Gloria. In this hymn of worship, praise, and thanksgiving we paraphrase the song of the angels in Luke 2:14, singing glory to God in the highest and peace to his people on earth. If the Gloria is not sung, it is to be recited by all together or in alternation.

The Opening Prayer or Collect

This prayer expresses the theme of the celebration, and, by the words of the priest, a petition is addressed to God the Father through the mediation of Christ in the Holy Spirit. Before this opening prayer, we are all invited to pray in silence. The priest then "collects" the assembly's prayer into a general prayer of praise and petition suited to the season or feast. The people's "amen" confirms the prayer thus offered in their name.

Liturgy of the Word

There can be neither Christian congregation nor liturgy without the Word of God being proclaimed. Three Scripture readings are proclaimed at each Sunday Mass, along with a responsorial psalm which is either sung or recited. The readings are generally "thematic." In other words, they harmonize together and relate to each other. The lectors who proclaim the readings should be people who feel called to this ministry and have a deep love for and faith in God's Word. The readings should be listened to with reverence and respect. They are a principal part of the liturgy.

During most of the year, the first reading is an Old Testament passage chosen for its relationship to the Gospel selection. During Easter season (leading up to Pentecost), however, the reading is taken from the Acts of the Apostles. The first reading is followed by a brief period of silent reflection and then the responsorial psalm, taken from the Book of Psalms. The psalm is also chosen for its relationship to the readings of the day. The psalm may be sung or spoken. If it is sung, a cantor usually sings the psalm verses and the congregation sings the response. If it is spoken, it is recited in this same responsorial style.

The second reading at Mass is taken from the New Testament letters. Scripture tells us that Paul's letters were read to all the brethren in the early church (1 Thessalonians 5:27). During the major seasons and on the greater feasts, this reading has a more intimate relationship with the other two. The second reading is also followed by a brief period of silent reflection.

Next comes the reading of the Gospel. The Gospels are especially sacred to Christians because they contain the recorded words of Jesus. In the Old Testament, when Ezra opened the book of God's word to read it to the people, all the people stood up (Nehemiah 8:5). Likewise, we show our special reverence for the Gospel by standing. We prepare to hear the Gospel by singing a Gospel acclamation (an Alleluia verse).

If a deacon is involved in the liturgy, the deacon reads the Gospel. To prepare him for this sacred privilege, the priest may give the deacon a blessing saying, "The Lord be in your heart and on your lips that you may worthily proclaim His Gospel." When there is no deacon, the priest reads the Gospel. Before doing so, he prays, "Almighty God, cleanse my heart and my lips that I may worthily proclaim your Gospel." This prayer is usually said privately by the priest.

As an alternative, the priest may say a longer form of the prayer out loud, based on Isaiah 6:

> Cleanse my heart and my lips, oh Almighty God, who cleansed the lips of the prophet Isaiah with a burning coal. In your gracious mercy, deign to purify me that I may worthily proclaim your holy Gospel. Through Christ Our Lord, amen.

The Gospel reader (deacon or priest) then introduces the Gospel with the words, "A reading from the Holy Gospel according to ———-. He makes the Sign of the Cross on the book with his thumb and then on his forehead, lips, and breast. The people also make the Sign of the Cross with their thumbs on their foreheads, lips, and breasts as a reminder that the Word of God is to be in our minds, on our lips, and in our hearts.

The Homily

After all the readings are completed, the people sit down and the priest gives a homily (sermon). The homily relates to the readings of the day and provides insights and practical applications for our daily lives. There are many gifted preachers in the Catholic Church today. I have been blessed to have some very Spirit-filled and prayerful Scripture scholars as pastors. One of them (Fr. Bohdan Kosicki) was a gifted artist as well. He always used illustrations and visual aids in his sermons. Needless to say, a good homily can be educational, edifying, and a real blessing to the listeners.

The Creed

The Creed is our profession of faith. Scripture tells us that we are to believe in our hearts that Jesus is Lord and confess it with our lips (Romans 10:9-10). We do that as we stand and recite our creed. The act of standing shows the unity of our faith. It shows our agreement with what is being professed and the fact that we will "stand up" for what we believe. Our creed is based on the Nicene Creed, which goes all the way back to the fourth century. It embodies all of the basic doctrines of the Christian faith. It is proclaimed out loud by the entire congregation. We say:

> We believe in one God, the Father, the Almighty, Maker of heaven and earth, of all that is seen and unseen. We believe in one Lord, Jesus Christ, the only Son of God, eternally begotten of the Father, God from God, light from light, true God from true God, begotten, not made, one in being with the Father. Through him all things were made. For us and for our salvation he came down from heaven. By the power of the Holy Spirit he was born of the Virgin Mary, and became man. For our sake he was crucified under Pontius Pilate; he suffered, died and was buried. On the third day, he rose again in fulfillment of the Scriptures; he ascended into heaven and is seated at the right hand of the Father. He will come again in glory to judge the living and the dead, and his kingdom will have no end. We believe in the Holy Spirit, the Lord, the Giver of life, who proceeds from the Father and the Son. With the Father and the Son he is worshipped and glorified. He has spoken through the prophets. We believe in one, holy catholic and apostolic Church. We acknowledge one baptism for the forgiveness of sins. We look for the resurrection of the dead, and the life of the world to come. Amen.

It is significant to note that the word "catholic" in our creed is not capitalized. It means universal. In other words, what we are saying is that we believe in the holy Christian and apostolic church. We believe in the Body of Christ here on earth, not just one denomination.

Petitions

The petitions are intercessory prayers for the needs of our sisters and brothers both in our local community and throughout the world. In accordance with Scripture, we pray for each other (James 5:16). We pray that people will respond to God's call to the priesthood, religious life, and lay ministries (Matthew 9:37-38). We pray for our priests and religious leaders (Ephesians 6:19; Colossians 4:3; 2 Thessalonians 3:1). We pray for missionaries (Acts 13:3). We pray for all fellow believers (Ephesians 6:18). The intercessions usually include the needs of the Church, public authorities, the salvation of the world, and those oppressed by any need. The deacon or lector prays each intention, and the congregation joins in agreement by responding, "Lord, hear our prayer." The priest then draws all the intentions together in a concluding prayer.

Preparation of the Altar and the Gifts

The altar table is set, and members of the community bring up bread and wine that will be consecrated and consumed in the Eucharist. The collection is taken up to support the liturgical and pastoral needs of the assembly and also to feed the poor. Philippians 4:18 speaks of offerings for the support of the ministry. Jesus spoke of offering our gifts at the altar (Matthew 5:23). The bread and wine that we offer symbolize our material goods, our works, and the fruits of our labor.

The offertory prayer is based on an ancient Hebrew, Old Testament prayer: "Blessed are you, God of all creation. Through your goodness we have this bread to offer, which earth has given and human hands have made. It will become for us the bread of life." The people respond, "Blessed be God forever." As the gifts are brought up and the collection is taken, the community prepares for the Eucharist in song or in silent prayer. The offertory prayer continues, "Blessed are you, God of all creation. Through your goodness we have this wine to offer, fruit of the vine and work of human hands. It will become our spiritual drink." Again, the congregation answers, "Blessed be God forever."

Eucharistic Prayer

The Eucharistic prayer is a prayer of praise, thanksgiving, and intercession leading up to the most important part of the Mass, the consecration. It is rooted in the ancient table prayers prayed by Jesus and his disciples. The Eucharistic prayer is one of the earliest Christian liturgies, described by Justin Martyr (d. 165 A.D.). In fact, the Eucharistic prayers used today are very similar to the one found in the Church order of Hippolytus (d. 236 A.D.). It begins with the following responsorial prayer:

Priest:	The Lord be with you.
People:	And also with you.
Priest:	Lift up your hearts.
People:	We lift them up to the Lord.
Priest:	Let us give thanks to the Lord our God.
People:	It is right to give him thanks and praise.

The Eucharistic prayer continues with the "preface." At the end of the preface prayer, the priest joins his hands and, together with the people, concludes by singing or saying aloud a song of praise that is found in Isaiah 6:3, Revelation 4:8, Psalm 118:26, and Matthew 21:9: "Holy, holy, holy Lord, God of power and might. Heaven and earth are full of your glory. Hosanna in the highest. Blessed is he who comes in the name of the Lord. Hosanna in the highest."

The priest then continues with the Eucharistic prayer chosen for the day, leading up to the consecration. The consecration is a reenactment of the Last Supper, when Jesus took bread, broke it, gave it to his disciples, and said, "Take this, all of you, and eat it. This is my body which is given up for you." Then he took the cup, gave it to his disciples, and said, "Take this, all of you, and drink from it. This is the cup of my blood, the blood of the new and everlasting covenant. It will be shed for you and for all so that sins may be forgiven. Do this in memory of me." Before repeating Jesus' sacred words, the priest prays that the bread and wine may become for us the body and blood of Jesus. (The significance of the Eucharist is discussed in Chapter 6.) After the consecration, the priest continues with the rest of the Eucharistic prayer in intercession for us, for the Church, for our leaders, for the community, and for our own private intentions.

The Communion Rite

The Communion Rite begins with the congregation praying the prayer that Jesus taught us in Matthew 6:9-13, the Our Father. It may be sung or recited. Needless to say, it is a beautiful, powerful prayer of praise, petition, and confession. In many Catholic churches, the congregation joins hands as a symbol of our unity in the Body of Christ, our fellowship, and our "communion."

The Sign of Peace

1 Thessalonians 5:26 tells us to "Greet all the brethren with a holy kiss." Indeed, this part of the Mass used to be called the "kiss of peace." Having prayed together as one people preparing to share the one bread and the one cup, we give outward expression of our communion and love for one another. We greet those around us with a handshake or a hug. The traditional greeting is "The peace of Christ be with you," and the response is "And also with you." Why do we use this specific greeting? Because the peace of Christ is a special kind of peace that only He can give. It is a peace that passes all understanding (Philippians 4:7), a peace that doesn't depend on our circumstances.

The Lamb of God

The Lamb of God is sung as an accompaniment to the breaking of the communion bread. We are reminded that Jesus is the sacrificial lamb of which the Passover lamb and the blood on the doorpost in Exodus were a type or symbol. Through the sacrifice of Jesus' body and blood, we have eternal life. Before receiving communion, we paraphrase the words of the centurion in Matthew 8:8: "Lord, I am not worthy to receive you, but only say the word and I shall be healed." A communion song is sung while the assembly, both priest and people, receive communion. Following communion, there is a period of silence for private prayer and meditation. During this time, a psalm or song of worship and adoration may be sung by the choir. Following this quiet time, the priest concludes the liturgy of the Eucharist with the prayer after communion.

Concluding Rite

The word Mass comes from the Latin word "Missa," meaning sent. And so, having been fed and nourished with the word of God and the Eucharist, we are now sent forth to love and serve the Lord. If there are any brief announcements, they may be made at this time. The rite of dismissal takes place, and the priest blesses the people. As the priest, Eucharistic ministers, lectors, and servers process out, a joyful, uplifting, recessional hymn is sung. As Isaiah 55:12 says, "You shall go out in joy, and be led forth in peace."

Symbolism

The Catholic Mass is rich in symbolism. Following is a description of some of the symbols and their scriptural relationships.

Vestments

In Exodus, God gave Moses specific directions for the making of holy garments for the priests (28:1-8, 14, 31-35). The garments were to be made for "glory and beauty" and to consecrate the priests. They were to be colorful, decorative, ornamental, and of fine materials. They were to be worn by the priests when they ministered in the holy place. In Numbers, God gave instructions to the people of Israel about wearing tassels to remind them of the commandments of the Lord (15:37-41).

Likewise, in the Catholic Church, the priest wears colorful, decorative vestments to remind him and us of various virtues and responsibilities. Different colors are worn for different seasons. White is used in the Masses of the Easter and Christmas seasons. Red is used on Passion Sunday (Palm Sunday), Good Friday, Pentecost, celebrations of the Passion, and birthday feasts of the apostles, evangelists, and martyrs. Green is used at the Masses during ordinary time. Violet is used in Lent and Advent. Rose may be used on the third Sunday of Advent and the fourth Sunday of Lent.

In the Body of Christ, not all members have the same function (Romans 12:4-8; 1 Corinthians 12:4-7). In the Catholic Church the diversity of ministries is shown externally in worship by the diversity of vestments. The vestment common to all ministers at the Mass is the alb, tied at the waste with a cincture, unless it is made to fit without a cincture. This garment is worn by the acolytes (servers), who assist the priest at Mass. The deacon wears the alb, stole, and dalmatic. The following is a specific description of the traditional vestments worn by the priest and what the vestments symbolize:

Amice - a white linen cloth worn around the neck of the priest and covering the shoulder. In the Middle Ages, it was worn over the head. It symbolizes the helmet of salvation (Ephesians 6:17).

Alb - the long, white linen garment symbolizing the innocence and purity that a priest should reflect.

Cincture - a cord used as a belt to gird the alb. It symbolizes the virtue of chastity and celibacy by which the priest is bound. It is also reminiscent of Ephesians 6:14: "Stand therefore, having girded your loins with truth."

Maniple - an ornamental vestment worn over the left forearm. It symbolizes the labor and hardship a priest must expect in his ministry.

Stole - a symbol of the official authority of a priest. Roman magistrates wore a long scarf when engaged in their official duties, just as our judges wear court gowns.

Chasuble - the colorful, decorative outer vestment put on over the others, symbolizing the virtue of charity and the yoke of service for the Lord, which the priest assumes at ordination. It reminds us of Jesus' words in Matthew 11:29: "Take my yoke upon you, and learn from me; for I am gentle and lowly in heart, and you will find rest for your souls."

Since Vatican II, the vestments have been simplified somewhat. The Amice and Maniple are no longer worn.

The Altar

In Exodus 20:24-26 and 27:1,8, God told Moses to build an altar and instructed him as to the specific dimensions and materials to be used. It was on the altar, of course, that the various offerings were to be made to God by the priest. Numbers chapter 7 tells of the dedication of the altar, which was to be a focal point of worship in the Old Testament. Likewise, the altar is a focal point of worship in the Catholic Church.

The Cross

The cross, of course, is the symbol of Christ's sacrifice on Calvary. There is always a cross or crucifix either on the altar or near it within the view of the congregation during Mass. The cross or crucifix may be carried in during the entrance procession. The crucifix portrays Jesus Christ crucified as a reminder of the horrible torture he went through for us (see Galatians 3:1). The empty cross emphasizes the resurrection. Both the cross and crucifix have their place in Christian faith and worship.

Candles

In the Old Testament God gave his people instructions about lamps to be placed around the altar (Numbers 8:1-4). In Zechariah 4:10, lamps were said to represent the eyes of the Lord, which range through the whole earth. Exodus 25:37 tells us that lamps were to be placed around the Ark of the Testimony so as to give light upon the space in front of it. In the Catholic Mass, we have candles situated around the altar in differing numbers according to the degree of the festivity. They also are a reminder of the eyes of God watching over us.

Exodus 25:31 speaks of one special lampstand of pure gold. Likewise, in the Catholic Church, we have one prominent candle called the Pascal candle, which represents the light of Christ. In a candlelight service in the Easter Vigil Mass, everyone in the congregation lights a candle from this Pascal candle, symbolizing our receiving and spreading of the light of Christ.

Incense

In Exodus 30:1,7-8 Moses is given instructions by God to burn incense on the altar. Leviticus 16:13 also speaks of this practice. The burning of incense continued in the New Testament. Zechariah (father of John the Baptist) was a priest who burned incense in the temple according to the custom of the priesthood at the hour of incense (Luke 1:8-10). In the Catholic Church, incense may be burned at Mass, particularly if it is a very formal Mass or an important feast day, such as the Easter Vigil Mass. The incense is a symbol of the Church's offerings and prayers going up to God.

Furnishings and Utensils

In Exodus, God instructs Moses to make a table. On the table would be the plates and dishes for incense, the bowls to pour libations, and the Bread of the Presence (Exodus 25:29-30). In the Catholic

Church, we also have a side table on which are kept the cruets of water and wine, the dish and towel for the symbolic washing of the priest's hands, the sacramentary book, and the chalice. The unconsecrated bread and wine for communion may also be kept there until they are carried up at the offertory.

Tabernacle

In Exodus Chapter 26, God instructs Moses in meticulous detail as to the construction and furnishing of the tabernacle. A great deal of time and space is spent in the Old Testament describing the tabernacle. In the tabernacle was the Ark of the Testimony, which was overlaid in pure gold (Exodus 25:10-11). In the Catholic Church, our tabernacle is also made of gold. In the tabernacle is kept the consecrated communion bread (our Bread of the Presence).

The Lamp

In Exodus 27:20–21, God tells Moses that a lamp shall be set up to burn continuously in the tent of meeting outside the veil that is before the testimony. In the Catholic Church, a candle is kept burning continuously when the Blessed Sacrament (consecrated bread) is present in the tabernacle.

The Washing of Hands

In Exodus 30:17–20, God instructs Moses that the priests are to wash their hands and their feet when they go into the tent of meeting or when they come near to the altar to minister and burn offerings. In the Catholic Mass, the priest performs the symbolic ritual of washing his hands as an expression of his desire for inward purification.

Sacrifice

In the Old Testament, the people were told to offer continual blood sacrifices on the altar in the tent of meeting. The animals sacrificed had to be perfect and without blemish (Leviticus 1:3, 10). Those sacrifices were types or symbols of the one perfect sacrifice that would be offered for our salvation—Jesus Christ, the Lamb of God.

The Mass also is sometimes referred to as a sacrifice. 1 Peter 2:4-5 tells us to be a holy priesthood and to offer spiritual sacrifices acceptable to God through Jesus Christ. This is what we do at Mass. We offer up a sacrifice of praise to God (Hebrews 13:15). We share what we have as a sacrifice pleasing to God (Hebrews 13:16). Most importantly, we commemorate Jesus' sacrifice for us on Calvary.

The Spirit-Filled Mass

Some Catholic Churches occasionally have special Masses, called charismatic Masses, where the gifts of the Holy Spirit are freely manifested (See more on this subject in Chapter 9). They are beautiful, uplifting, Spirit-filled Masses, and I highly recommend them. In my opinion, however, every Mass should be a Spirit-filled, charismatic Mass. We should worship "in spirit and in truth" (John 4:24). The gifts of the Holy Spirit should be exercised, provided we meet the requirement of 1 Corinthians 14:40, that all things should be done decently and in order. There are a number of things we can do within the context of every Catholic Mass to make it a more Spirit-filled, charismatic celebration.

When the priest says, "The Lord be with you," and we answer, "And also with you," we can extend our hands toward him and lift him up to the Lord in prayer. During the penitential rite, we can ask the Holy Spirit to convict us of any sin in our lives and then confess it and repent so as to cleanse ourselves in preparation for communion. We can personalize the prayers. When we say "Lord, have mercy," we can privately add some specific person or thing we are asking the Lord's mercy for. We can expand upon the responses. For example, when the response is "Thanks be to God," we can continue thanking God for a few moments privately.

During the readings, we should listen very intently. We should ask the Lord to show us what He is saying specifically to us during the readings. If possible, we should read the Scripture readings of the day and meditate on them before Mass. During the homily, we should listen to the priest's insights on the Word of God. If anything especially hits home, we should take notes. During the Creed, we should sincerely reaffirm the elements of our Christian faith. We should concentrate on what Jesus did to save us.

During the offertory, the presentation of the gifts, we should consciously offer ourselves to God as a living sacrifice, offering back to God everything he has given to us: our home, our family, our money, our possessions. As we pray the prayer of the faithful, we should really pay attention to every petition and lift it up to the Lord. We can pray quietly in tongues at this time as well. When the priest says, "Lift up your hearts," and we respond, "We lift them up to the Lord," we can lift our hands up to the Lord as a symbolic gesture that we are giving Him our prayers, our needs, our body, soul, mind and spirit.

When we sing the "holy, holy, holy," we should put our whole heart and soul into it. We should see ourselves at the throne of God with all the angels and saints, and really sing it to God, not just as a ritual. When we sing the Great Amen, we should realize that we are joining in the Eucharistic prayer of the priest and making it our personal prayer of praise, thanksgiving, petition, and contrition.

When we pray the Our Father, we can join hands with the people on either side of us to show our unity in the Spirit and to make it a true community prayer. It is a fairly simple gesture, but it makes the Lord's Prayer a very powerful and moving experience. At the consecration, we should acknowledge Jesus' presence and praise Him and thank Him for this gift and for sacrificing His body and blood for us.

At the greeting of peace, we can pray that God will touch and minister to each person we touch and greet. We can pray that they will truly experience the peace of Christ, which passes all understanding. At Holy Communion, we can read and meditate on Scriptures such as 1 Corinthians 11:23-29. We can ask Jesus to help us receive Him in a worthy manner, properly discerning His presence. This is the holiest and most sacred time of Mass. It is an opportunity for us to enter into private, intimate prayer and meditation with the Lord. We can bow our heads, close our eyes, cover our faces with our hands, and praise and thank Jesus quietly in English and/or tongues as the Spirit prompts us. Then we can join in the communion song, which is a form of community praise and thanksgiving.

After the communion song, during the quiet reflection time, we can listen for the Lord's word (prophecy). If we feel that we receive a word from the Lord, we can share it with others after Mass if we feel led to do so.

The gift of healing can be exercised during the penitential rite and during the sign of peace. During communion, as we see our friends and family members receiving the Eucharist, we can pray that God will touch them and heal them. The gift of tongues can be exercised quietly before and after the entrance song, during the Eucharistic prayer, during the quiet times, at the consecration (praising God), and during the priest's prayer before the doxology portion of the Our Father.

Thus, the Mass can be a very beautiful, scriptural, deep, moving, spiritual, and Spirit-filled worship experience. In fact, it can be a life-changing experience. Many people first experience the presence of Jesus at Mass and accept Him as their Lord and Savior. But Mass is not a "spectator sport." In order to get anything out of it, we must participate. We must really enter into it with our body, soul, mind and spirit.

"You shall build an alter to the Lord your God... and you shall sacrifice peace offereings, and you shall eat there; and you shall rejoice before the Lord your God." (Deuteronomy 27:6-7)

CHAPTER VI

The Eucharist

Our Emmanuel

Jesus is present where two or three are gathered in His name (Matthew 18:20). He is present in the church, His body here on earth. He is present in His Word. The Word is living and active. He is the Word made flesh (John 1:14). Jesus is also present in a very special, personal, and intimate way when we receive Him as our spiritual food in communion.

Jesus sacrificed His body for us on Calvary. Through the Eucharist we can partake of that sacrifice and actually have His body within us. The blood of Jesus is our most powerful weapon against the devil. We are justified by the blood of Jesus (Romans 5:9). It is the blood of Jesus that cleanses us from all sin (1 John 1:7). There's healing, protection and forgiveness in the blood of Jesus. As an old song puts it, "There is power, power, wonder working power in the precious blood of the Lamb." Through the Eucharist we can actually have the blood of Jesus within us. What a precious and awesome gift!

To Catholics, the Eucharist is "Emmanuel," God with us. It is the climax of our liturgy. It is essential to our spiritual health; our relationship to God. Along with the Word of God, the Eucharist is a central aspect of our faith. It is the essence of Catholic Christianity.

The importance of the Eucharist is shown by the fact that in the early church, the liturgy was actually called the "breaking of the bread." In Acts 2:42 we read, "And they devoted themselves to the Apostles' teaching and fellowship, to the breaking of bread and the prayers." This is what Catholics do in the Mass. We devote ourselves to the apostles' teaching in the liturgy of the Word and the homily, we devote ourselves to fellowship with other believers, we devote ourselves to the breaking of the bread in the Eucharist, and we devote ourselves to prayers of repentance, praise, intercession, and worship. We believe that every Christian liturgy should include these four elements: preaching and teaching of the word, Christian fellowship, prayers, and the

Eucharist (communion). Without any one of these elements, the liturgy is incomplete.

Old Testament References

The Old Testament speaks in several places of the "Bread of God" or "Bread of the Presence" (see Leviticus 21:8, 17, 22; Numbers 4:7; 1 Samuel 21:6). In the New Testament, the writer of Hebrews comments,

> Now even the first covenant had regulations for worship and an earthly sanctuary. For a tent was prepared, the outer one, in which were the lamp stand and the table and the bread of the Presence; it is called the Holy Place. Behind the second curtain stood a tent called the Holy of Holies, having the golden altar of incense and the ark of the covenant covered on all sides with gold, which contained a golden urn holding the manna, and Aaron's rod that budded, and the tables of the covenant; above it were the cherubim of glory overshadowing the mercy seat. Of these things we cannot now speak in detail. (9:1-5)

Jesus also refers to the "Bread of the Presence" in Luke 6:3-4 and Mark 2:25-26.

What was this sacred "Bread of the Presence" of the Old Testament? I believe it was a type or symbol of the true Bread of the Presence in the New Testament—Jesus' body and blood given to us in communion. Jesus is the Bread of the Presence for the Church today.

In the Old Testament Passover meal, I believe we have another great type or symbol of the Eucharist. Jesus specifically chose the Passover meal for the inauguration of the Eucharist (Luke 22:15). Compare the Old Testament Passover (Exodus 12:1-13) to the Last Supper in the New Testament. The people in the Old Testament were instructed not only to kill the lamb and put its blood on their doorposts but also to eat the lamb. Jesus is our Passover lamb. At communion we say, "Lamb of God, you take away the sins of the world; have mercy on us." The communion bread is Jesus' body, our Passover lamb, and we are not only to reverence it, we are to consume it.

The Passover was a special meal (Exodus 12:43-49). No foreigner was to eat of it. Likewise, our Eucharistic meal is very special. It is not to be shared with nonbelievers, unless they convert. The Passover meal was a reminder of what God had done for the Jewish people (Exodus 13:9). Our Eucharistic meal reminds us what Jesus did for us. He has delivered us from the bondage of sin just as God delivered the Israelites from the bondage of slavery. Jesus is the blood on our doorposts to preserve us from spiritual death and give us eternal life. At the Passover, a special bread (unleavened) was used. Leaven represents sin. Unleavened bread is pure (Exodus 13:7). We use unleavened bread for communion because Jesus is pure and sinless.

If Jesus' body becomes part of ours, we are in a sense part of the body that was sacrificed for our sins. We become, as Paul puts it, "a living sacrifice" (Romans 12:1). I believe the Eucharist is a very deep, deep subject. We probably will not fully understand its significance until we get to heaven. It has to do with our very salvation and the spiritual warfare between God and Satan. Maybe that is why there has been so much controversy over the Eucharist for so many years—Satan doesn't want Christians to discover how powerful the Eucharist really is.

Our Manna

In John 6:48-51, Jesus likens Himself to the manna given to the children of Israel in the wilderness:

> I am the Bread of Life. Your fathers ate the manna in the wilderness, and they died. This is the bread which comes down from heaven, that a man may eat of it and not die. I am the living bread which came down from heaven; if anyone eats of this bread, he will live forever; and the bread which I shall give for the life of the world is my flesh.

Manna actually means "what is it?" (Exodus 16:14-15). This is still the question for many Christians today concerning the Eucharist. What exactly is it? What is its significance? Moses answered the people in the Old Testament, "It is the bread which the Lord has given you to eat" (Exodus 16:15). Jesus answers the question for us in the words of the consecration: "Take, eat; this is my body" (Matthew 26:26; Mark 14:22).

After the Israelites entered into Canaan, they no longer ate manna; they ate the fruit of the land (Joshua 5:10-12). Likewise, we will eat our manna (communion) until Jesus returns and establishes His kingdom and we enter our Canaan land. We won't need communion then because we will see Him face to face. One of our communion acclamations at Mass is "When we eat this Bread and drink this Cup we proclaim your death Lord Jesus, *until* you come in glory."

What Did Jesus Say?

At the Last Supper, Jesus took bread and said, "This is my body," not "This is a symbol of my body or a representation of my body." Jesus' words of the Eucharist were so specific and explicit that many of his disciples quit following him after he explained it (John 6:66).

In John 6:32-33, Jesus says, "Truly, truly, I say to you, it was not Moses who gave you the bread from heaven; my Father gives you the true bread from heaven. For the bread of God is that which comes down from heaven, and gives life to the world." His disciples replied, "Lord, give us this bread always" (John 6:34).

In the Eucharist, Jesus does give us this bread always. In Matthew 28:20, He says, "Lo, I am with you always, to the close of the age." In John 14:19-20, He says, "Yet a little while, and the world will see me no more, but you will see me; because I live, you will live also. In that day you will know that I am in my Father, and you in me, and I in you." The world does not see Jesus in the Eucharist, but we Christians do. Through the Eucharist we know that we are in Jesus and He is in us.

A beautiful illustration of recognizing Jesus in the Eucharist is given in the account of Jesus and the disciples on their way to Emmaus after the Resurrection (Luke 24:13-35). As they walked with the risen Lord down the road to Emmaus, they did not recognize Him. He discussed the Scriptures with them and interpreted the Old Testament passages referring to Him. Thus, in effect, they had the liturgy of the Word. They still did not recognize Him. Later, at table, He took bread, blessed it, and broke it and gave it to them. At that point, verse 31 says, "And their eyes were opened and they recognized him; and he vanished out of their sight." They recognized Jesus in the breaking of the bread (Luke 24:35). Reading and explaining the Word of God alone is not enough.

The Eucharist is an opportunity for us to recognize Jesus and His kingdom in the breaking of the bread.

In John 6:35 Jesus says, "I am the bread of life; he who comes to me shall not hunger, and he who believes in me shall never thirst." Jesus alone can satisfy our spiritual hunger and thirst. Without Him we are empty, no matter what else we may possess. We cling to life, but only in Jesus can we have eternal life. In John 6:53–54, Jesus says, "Truly, truly, I say to you, unless you eat the flesh of the Son of man and drink his blood, you have no life in you; he who eats my flesh and drinks my blood has eternal life, and I will raise him up at the last day." In Jesus and in the Eucharist we have the promise of eternal life and our own personal resurrection.

Jesus made it clear that his flesh and blood are food and drink and if we partake of this food and drink, we will abide in Him. In John 6:55-58 He says,

> For my flesh is food indeed, and my blood is drink indeed. He who eats my flesh and drinks my blood abides in me, and I in him. As the living Father sent me, and I live because of the Father, so he who eats me will live because of me. This is the bread which came down from heaven, not such as the fathers ate and died; he who eats this bread will live for ever.

In summary, Jesus tells us that this is His body, not a symbol or a representation of His body. He is the living bread come down from heaven. His flesh is real food; His blood is real drink. If we eat His body and drink His blood, He will abide in us and we will abide in Him. We will have eternal life and He will raise us up on the last day. But if we do not eat His body and drink His blood, we have no life in us. At the Last Supper, Jesus commanded us to do this in memory of Him. In view of these mandates, I frankly do not understand Christian churches that do not incorporate the Eucharist into their liturgies. I do not understand Christian churches that do not serve communion at every liturgy.

What Did Paul Say?

In Paul's first letter to the Corinthians, he gives us some great insight as to the meaning and understanding of the Eucharist in the early church. In 1 Corinthians 10:16, he says, "The cup of blessing which we bless, is it not a participation in the blood of Christ? The bread which we break, is it not a participation in the body of Christ?" He doesn't say it is a symbol of the body of Christ and the blood of Christ. He says it is an actual participation in the body of Christ and the blood of Christ. In Chapter 11 verses 23–30 he goes on to say:

> For I received from the Lord what I also delivered to you, that the Lord Jesus on the night when he was betrayed took bread, and when he had given thanks, he broke it, and said, "This is my body which is for you. Do this in remembrance of me." In the same way also the cup, after supper, saying, "This cup is the new covenant in my blood. Do this as often as you drink it, in remembrance of me." For as often as you eat this bread and drink the cup, you proclaim the Lord's death until he comes. Whoever, therefore, eats the bread or drinks the cup of the Lord in an unworthy manner will be guilty of profaning the body and blood of the Lord. Let a man examine himself, and so eat of the bread and drink of the cup. For anyone who eats and drinks without discerning the body eats and drinks judgment upon himself. That is why many of you are weak and ill, and some have died.

So we see that Paul repeats to the Corinthians what he has received from the Lord, namely, that the night before he died, Jesus took bread and said, "This is my body." Paul warns the Corinthians that if they eat the bread or drink the cup of the Lord in an unworthy manner, they will be guilty of profaning the very body and blood of the Lord. We also, therefore, should examine ourselves and make sure that we receive communion in a proper manner. We must be sure we discern that it is the body of Christ we are receiving.

Paul's statement to the Corinthians indicates that the reason why some of them were sick and had even died was their lack of understanding, discernment, and reverence for the Eucharist. The positive side of this statement would be that if we do receive the Eucharist with a proper understanding, discernment, and reverence for it, it can bring healing into our lives. Anyone needing a healing of any kind should receive communion with a proper understanding, discernment, and reverence for the Eucharist and with the specific intention of receiving healing. I believe there is healing power in the Eucharist when it is properly received. In fact, our Catholic prayer before receiving communion is "Lord, I am not worthy to receive you, but only say the word and I shall be healed."

Conclusion

Yes, we Catholics believe that the Eucharist is Jesus present among us. It is not just a symbol; it is Jesus. I know that separates us from some of our Protestant brothers and sisters, but so be it. When Jesus announced that we would have to eat His body and drink His blood, a lot of people couldn't take it; they left Him. It was controversial. But that was what He said and He didn't retract it, alter it or soften it. He didn't tell the people who left Him that they misunderstood, because they didn't. He obviously meant what He said. The Eucharist is food for our soul. It is spiritual nourishment. We need it just as we need His Word and the Holy Spirit within us. We need to really repent if we have taken this precious gift for granted. We need to really thank God for giving Himself to us in this wonderful way.

"For my flesh is food indeed, and my blood is drink indeed." (John 6:55)

CHAPTER VII

Traditions

Do We Really Need Them?

I love the introduction to the song "Tradition" from *Fiddler on the Roof.* Tevye says,

> Here in Anatevka we have traditions for everything: how to sleep, how to eat, how to work, how to wear clothes. For instance, we always keep our heads covered and always wear a little prayer shawl. This shows our constant devotion to God. You may ask, how did this tradition get started? I'll tell you. I don't know! But it's tradition; and because of our traditions, every one of us knows who he is and what God expects him to do.

In the pre-Vatican II Church I grew up in, we also had traditions for everything: how to sleep (before going to bed at night, we knelt down and prayed a whole series of prayers including the Our Father, Hail Mary, Glory Be, Angel of God, Act of Contrition, and a litany of God blesses); how to eat (we couldn't eat meat on Friday, couldn't eat for three hours before communion, couldn't drink any liquids for one hour before communion, couldn't eat candy during Lent); how to work (no working or shopping on Sundays); how to wear clothes (women had to keep their heads covered in church, nuns wore habits, we wore cloth scapulars with wool backing that slightly irritated our skin—like a mini version of the hair shirts people wore as penance in the Bible). We genuflected when entering church. The Mass was in Latin. We sang songs in Gregorian chant, etc. If you had asked me as a child how all these traditions got started, I would have told you the same thing as Tevye—I don't know! But because of our traditions, I sure knew I was Catholic—and so did everyone else.

In the pre-Vatican II Church, we had prayers for every occasion: morning prayers, evening prayers, prayers before meals, prayers after meals, prayers before Mass, prayers before communion, prayers after Mass and communion, prayers against persecutors and evildoers, prayers for times of trouble, prayers for any necessity, prayers for those in temptation and trouble, prayers for our friends, acts of faith, hope, love and contrition, and so on. At 6:00 a.m., 12:00 noon, and 6:00 p.m., the Catholic Church bells would ring and the Annunciation prayer (Angelus) would be said. Every time we went past a church, we were supposed to say a prayer or at least make the Sign of the Cross. To say that there were many opportunities and many reminders to pray in the pre-Vatican II Church would be an understatement.

The traditional prayers of the pre-Vatican II Church were very beautiful. The problem is that we generally "said them" rather than praying them from the heart. The current trend in the post-Vatican II Church is toward more spontaneous prayer. It is simpler—not always as profound or beautiful, but more sincere. The best prayers are those that come from our own hearts in our own words (or in tongues).

The Church still has traditional prayers for various occasions and situations. We can adopt these prayers and make them our own by praying them sincerely from the heart rather than simply rattling them off. We still have liturgical prayers and traditional "leader and response" prayers that are very effective for community worship. 2 Maccabees 1:23 illustrates that this practice is not new: "And while the sacrifice was being consumed, the priests offered prayer—the priests and every one. Jonathan led, and the rest responded, as did Nehemiah" (RSV). The post-Vatican II Church really doesn't tell us when or how often to pray, but 1 Thessalonians 5:17 does. It is one of the shortest verses in the Bible. It simply says, "Pray constantly." Hopefully, we will take this verse to heart.

Since Vatican II, some of our traditions have changed and others have been discontinued, but we are still a very traditional church. Is this good or bad? It depends. In Matthew 15:6, Jesus scolded the Pharisees, saying, "So for the sake of your tradition, you have made void the word of God." We know, however, that Jesus followed the religious traditions of His day and at times emphasized their importance. The question then is whether our traditions make void the Word of God. Are we concentrating on rigid enforcement of our rules and traditions while ignoring the Word of God? That is what Jesus criticized the Pharisees for. Are we trusting in our traditions to save us instead of trusting in Jesus

Christ? If we are, we are wrong. But if our traditions support our worship and faith, they are good.

Many Catholic traditions have been misunderstood, criticized and condemned by non-Catholics as being "unscriptural." It is important to remember that just because something may not be specifically mentioned in the Bible, it is not necessarily unscriptural. I doubt that many people would say it is unscriptural to say the Pledge of Allegiance to the flag or to sing the "Star-Spangled Banner." These things aren't found in the Bible. Likewise, there are some Protestant traditions, such as the "sinners' prayer" and the altar call that are not specifically mentioned in Scripture, but they are not unscriptural unless they conflict with Scripture. In this chapter then, I would like to examine some of the misunderstood and criticized Catholic traditions and, hopefully, demonstrate that they are not unscriptural.

Christianized Judaism

I once heard a person say that Roman Catholicism is simply "Christianized Judaism." As I thought about the statement, I came to the conclusion that there was actually some truth to it. In fact, isn't that what Christianity itself is? Our God is the God of Abraham, Isaac, and Jacob. Our Old Testament is the same as the Jewish Bible. The Jews were God's chosen people. Many of their traditions and rituals were specifically ordained by God. Our roots are in Judaism. The first Christians were all Jews. Jesus himself was a Jew.

Actually, the early Christians wanted to make all converts become Jewish and go through the ritual of circumcision. They wanted to make them keep the dietary laws. There was quite a dispute in the early church over this. The early Christians attended the synagogue and taught and preached there until they were prohibited from doing so. Acts 5:42 says, "And every day in the temple and at home they did not cease teaching and preaching Jesus as the Christ."

There are many parallels between Old Testament Judaism and Catholicism. We have already discussed the relationship of the manna and the Bread of the Presence to our Eucharist. We have discussed the relationship of our altar and tabernacle to the Old Testament altar and tabernacle. We have discussed the relationship of the Old Testament sacrifices to the New Testament sacrifice of Jesus and our commemoration of that sacrifice in the Mass. The Catholic Church has, indeed, taken many of the Old Testament Jewish traditions and "Christianized" them, giving them Christian symbolism and meaning. Perhaps the reason the Catholic Church retains more of the Old Testament rituals and symbols than some other denominations is that our Church dates back to Apostolic times. We must remember that all Scripture, Old Testament and New, is inspired by God. If God taught us how to worship in the Old Testament, why shouldn't we incorporate that teaching into our New Testament worship?

The Early Church

Contrary to what some people may think, tradition was not a dirty word in the early Christian church. Scripture clearly reveals that Jesus followed the Old Testament traditions. When He cleansed a leper in Mark 1:44, He told the leper to perform the ritual of going and showing himself to the priest and offering for his cleansing what Moses commanded. Jesus' family followed the Jewish traditions. They took him to Jerusalem to present him to the Lord and to offer sacrifice according to the law (Luke 2:22-24). Jesus' position on tradition is clearly stated in Matthew 5:17-19:

> Think not that I have come to abolish the law and the prophets; I have not come to abolish them but to fulfill them. For truly, I say to you, till heaven and earth pass away, not an iota, not a dot, will pass from the law until all is accomplished. Whoever then relaxes one of the least of these commandments and teaches men so, shall be called least in the kingdom of heaven; but he who does them and teaches them shall be called great in the kingdom of heaven.

Traditions in the early church included such things as prayers, fasting, laying on of hands, and the breaking of the bread (see Acts 2:42). Acts 3:1 tells us that Peter and John followed the tradition of going up to the temple at the "hour of prayer," the ninth hour. Paul says in 1 Corinthians 11:2, "I commend you because you remember me in everything and maintain the traditions even as I have delivered them to you." 2 Thessalonians 2:15 says, "So then, brethren, stand firm and hold to the traditions which you were taught by us, either by word of mouth or by letter." And 2 Thessalonians 3:6 warns us, "Now we command you, brethren, in the name of our Lord Jesus Christ, that you keep away from any brother who is living in idleness and not in accord with the tradition that you have received from us." So tradition developed along with the Word of God. Both were important in the early church, and both are important in the Catholic Church today.

What About Sacraments?

The Catholic Church is a sacramental church. Sacraments are outward signs of God's grace. Through them, we encounter Jesus Christ at important and crucial moments in our lives. These are moments when we are confronted with the basic issues of life and God: Baptism (birth), reconciliation (forgiveness and conversion), communion (receiving Jesus), confirmation (coming into adulthood), anointing of the sick (sickness, healing, and death), marriage and holy orders (vocational decisions and lifelong commitments). In the sacraments, we use natural elements such as water, fire, and oils as symbols. Water symbolizes life; we cannot survive without it. Fire symbolizes power and mystery; it gives us light and warmth. Oil symbolizes something rich, precious, pure and holy; it is also a resource, a fuel, a source of energy. In the sacraments, Jesus purifies us as water purifies us. He enlightens us as fire gives us light. The Holy Spirit within us is our spiritual fuel.

God used these same natural elements in connection with many miraculous events in the Bible. The Angel spoke to Moses from a burning bush in Exodus 3:2. Fire came down from heaven as a sign in answer to the prayer of Elijah in 1 Kings 18:38. Tongues as of fire came upon the disciples at Pentecost (Acts 2:3). God provided water from the rock in Exodus 17:5-7 and Numbers 20:7-11. Naaman's leprosy was cured after washing seven times in the River Jordan (2 Kings 5:10-14). Jesus changed water into wine (John 2:1-11) and walked on water (John 6:19-20). In healing the man born blind, Jesus actually used saliva and then told the man to "go, wash in the pool of Siloam" (John 9:1-7). The widow's oil was increased in 1 Kings 17:14-16 and 2 Kings 4:2-7.

In the Old Testament, anointing with oil was a symbol of God's approval of a person for the office he was to fulfill. Priests were anointed (Exodus 30:30). Kings were annointed(1 Samuel 16:12-13). Even the holy things of the temple were anointed (Exodus 30:25-29). We continue this tradition in the anointing of priests in the sacrament of holy orders. We also use anointing with oil in the sacrament of the sick. This is in accordance with James 5:14, which says, "Is any among you sick? Let him call for the elders of the church, and let them pray over him, anointing him with oil in the name of the Lord." Anointing with oil is also done in the sacraments of baptism and confirmation.

Another symbol used in the sacraments is the laying on of hands. This again is consistent with the traditions of the early church. The laying on of hands accompanied receiving the Holy Spirit in the early church (Acts 8:17; 19:6) and receiving the gifts of the Holy Spirit (1 Timothy 4:14; 2 Timothy 1:6); thus in the Catholic Church, we have the laying on of hands with the sacrament of confirmation. In the early church, the laying on of hands accompanied the appointment of ministers (Acts 6:6; 13:3); thus in the Catholic Church, we have the laying on of hands with the sacrament of holy orders (ordination). And, of course, there are many instances in the Bible where touch and laying on of hands were used in connection with miraculous healing; thus, we have the laying on of hands with the sacrament of the sick and in simply praying over people for healing.

Perhaps the most controversial sacrament in the Catholic Church is reconciliation, sometimes called penance or confession. This could be because there is so much healing, forgiveness, and conversion in this sacrament that the enemy wants to detract from it as much as possible. Since Vatican II, the sacrament of reconciliation can be received in private confession form or, under some circumstances, in a group or communal form. If we have a personal problem we want to discuss with a priest or we want some spiritual advice, or we just want a priest to give us personal absolution and to declare to us that our sins are "absolutely" forgiven, then private confession is always available.

But is the sacrament of reconciliation scriptural? I would certainly say it is. James 5:6 tells us, "Therefore confess your sins to one another, and pray for one another, that you may be healed. The prayer of a righteous man has great power in its effects." 1 Timothy 6:12 tells us to "fight the good fight of faith; take hold of the eternal life to which you were called when you made the good confession in the presence of many witnesses." Galatians 6:1 says, "Brethren, if a man is overtaken in any trespass, you who are spiritual should restore him in a spirit of gentleness. Look to yourself, lest you too be tempted." 2 Corinthians 5:19-20 tells us that God has entrusted to us the message and ministry of reconciliation. Acts 19:18 is an example of confession in the early church: "Many also of those who were now believers came, confessing and divulging their practices."

The authority of the priest to declare absolution (forgiveness of sins) is derived from Jesus' words to his disciples after his resurrection: "And when he had said this, he breathed on them, and said to them, 'Receive the Holy Spirit, if you forgive the sins of any, they are forgiven; if you retain the sins of any they are retained'" (John 20:22-23). Also, in Matthew 16:19, Jesus tells Peter, "I will give you the keys of the kingdom of heaven, and whatever you bind on earth shall be bound in heaven, and whatever you loose on earth shall be loosed in heaven." This authority was extended to all the disciples in Matthew 18:18, thus extending it by implication to all priests.

Lent

Why do Catholics fast during Lent? There are many references to fasting throughout the Bible. In Old Testament times, the king would sometimes declare a community fast, especially to hear from the Lord in dangerous situations (see 2 Chronicles 20:1-30 for a great example of this). Fasting also goes hand in hand with repentance (see Joel 2:12, 15). Fasting goes along with worshiping the Lord (Acts 13:2-3). It helps us to make our worship and praise more effective and more spiritual. Thus, we fast one hour before communion. Fasting goes along with seeking God's direction in appointing church leaders (Acts 14:23).

Fasting is not for God; it is for us. God doesn't benefit from it. It doesn't earn us favors (Isaiah 58:1-7). Fasting is spiritually beneficial to us for several reasons. First of all, disciplining the flesh increases our self-control. It makes us stronger spiritually and more open to receiving revelation from God. It helps us to hear from God at times of important decisions or in dangerous or difficult situations. It is also healthy from a physical standpoint. Our body is the temple of the Holy Spirit and we need to take care of it and try to make it look presentable.

The Catholic Church recognizes the spiritual benefits of fasting; therefore, we fast as a community during the 40 days of Lent, just as Jesus fasted 40 days in the desert (Matthew 4:2). Forty is a symbolic number in the Bible. In Genesis 7:12, it rained for 40 days. In Exodus 24:18, Moses was on the mountain for 40 days. The children of Israel wandered in the desert for 40 years. Our Lenten tradition is a season of penance to help us prepare spiritually for Easter. We are asked to abstain from meat on Ash Wednesday and the Fridays of Lent and to fast (meaning the two lesser meals are not to exceed the main meal) on Ash Wednesday and Good Friday. Other than that, the Church pretty much leaves it up to us as to when and how we fast.

Another tradition in connection with Lent is receiving ashes on the forehead on Ash Wednesday. The ashes remind us of our mortality. (Psalm 103:14: "For he knows our frame; he remembers that we are dust.") In biblical times when people repented, they wore sackcloth and put ashes on their heads. Jesus refers to this practice in Matthew 11:21. Thus, ashes on our foreheads also symbolize repentance.

The Catholic Church also celebrates the season of Advent in preparation for Christmas. During Advent we have the Advent wreath in church. Many families also have an Advent wreath with the four Advent candles in their home. The candles may be lit at dinnertime along with a prayer service and Scripture reading. Another Advent tradition is the Jesse tree, wherein each person takes a tag off the tree every day during Advent. The tags have written on them various nice things to do for someone. Other Advent traditions include making Advent calendars and banners. These traditions help us to concentrate on the spiritual meaning of Christmas rather than falling into the commercialization trap.

The Catholic Church also has special feast days and holy days, just as there were feast days and holy days in the Old Testament and in the early New Testament church. In the Old Testament, they had feasts such as Unleavened Bread, Harvest, and Ingathering (Exodus 23:14-16). The Feast of Pentecost was celebrated in the early church (1 Corinthians 16:8), as was the Feast of Unleavened Bread(Acts 20:6). Another feast was the dedication of the temple (John 10:22). Leviticus chapter 23 deals with the appointed feasts of the Lord, which were to be proclaimed as holy convocations. Thus, there is ample scriptural authority for special religious feast days or holy days. Our Catholic feast days and holy days celebrate significant events in Christianity and honor some of our faith heroes.

Other Traditions

A number of other Catholic traditions have been misunderstood, challenged, or questioned. This section discusses some of these traditions and what the Bible says about them.

Praying for the Dead

Why do Catholics pray for dead people? Does it do any good? I suppose we won't really know for sure until we get to heaven. We can't prove it does; we can't prove it doesn't. But I certainly don't think it can do any harm. 1 John 5:16 tells us we can intercede with God to forgive other people's sins: "If anyone sees his brother committing what is not a mortal sin, he will ask, and God will give him life for those whose sin is not mortal." So apparently it is not wrong to pray that God will give eternal life to someone whose sin is not mortal. Paul even spoke of people being baptized on behalf of the dead in 1 Corinthians 15:29. Apparently, he allowed for this practice in view of the fact that we will all be raised from the dead eventually. Suppose that a Christian is living in sin at the time of his death. He has accepted Christ as his Lord and Savior and has not committed the mortal sin of rejecting Jesus. Why not pray for that person in the hope that it might do some good? Catholic or not, you don't have to pray for the dead if you don't want to. But there is scriptural authority for doing so.

Purgatory

The issue of purgatory ties in with the previous issue of praying for the dead. If a person's soul is either in heaven or hell, it wouldn't do much good to pray for them. But the Bible actually speaks of three places where people go after they die. The first place is heaven, which we are all familiar with. The second place is hell (or Gehenna), which is the lake of fire reserved for the devil and all who follow him. The third place is called Hades, or the "abode of the dead." Although the word purgatory is not specifically used in the Bible, it could be the place referred to as Hades. Again, if a person is a Christian and has accepted Jesus Christ as his Lord and Savior but then backslides and is living in serious sin at the time of his death, where does he go? He isn't ready for heaven, but does he deserve hell?

In 1 Corinthians 3:13-15, Paul speaks of our works being tested by fire. If our works are laid on the foundation of Jesus Christ, they will survive this test and we will receive a reward. But if our works are burned up in this test, we will suffer loss, but we will be saved only "as through fire." This seems to imply a place of purging. In the parable of the faithful and wise steward (Luke 12:41-48), Jesus speaks of some people receiving a severe punishment and others receiving a light punishment. Perhaps, therefore, there are varying degrees of reward and punishment after death. Ultimately, we will all end up either in heaven or in hell, but we certainly cannot rule out a waiting place or purging place such as purgatory.

Relics

Relics (bone chips of dead saints, etc.) are not as popular now as they were in the pre-Vatican II Church, but the idea of relics having some spiritual or miraculous power could relate to Scriptures such as Acts 19:11–12: "And God did extraordinary miracles by the hands of Paul, so that handkerchiefs or aprons were carried away from his body to the sick, and diseases left them and the evil spirits came out of them." Some modern evangelists refer to "points of contact," "prayer cloths," etc. The Catholic Church does not emphasize relics, but we cannot say that the idea is unscriptural.

Stigmata

This is another concept that is hardly ever mentioned since Vatican II. It refers to people actually receiving the wounds of Christ in their bodies. Tradition tells us that several saints received this manifestation. I don't know if Paul was one such saint, but he does say in Galatians 6:17, "Henceforth let no man trouble me; for I bear on my body the marks of Jesus."

Apparitions

The idea of apparitions or visions of angels, saints, etc. is also looked upon with a great deal of skepticism by many people. Apparitions, however, are nothing new. In Acts 26:12-18, Jesus appeared to

Paul as he traveled to Damascus. It was through this vision that Paul was converted. In Matthew 17:3 and Luke 9:30, Moses and Elijah appeared to Jesus, Peter, James, and John. There are many other references in the Old and New Testaments to angels appearing to people with various messages at various times.

Mortal vs. Non-mortal Sins

The Church has traditionally referred to some sins as mortal and others as non-mortal, or venial. As indicated under the heading "Praying for the Dead," there is a scriptural basis for this distinction. 1 John 5:17 says, "All wrongdoing is sin, but there is sin which is not mortal."

Exorcism

The Catholic Church even has a ceremony for deliverance from evil spirits. Is this scriptural? Acts 16:16-18 tells us of a slave girl with a "spirit of divination" (fortune telling). She followed Paul, crying out, "These men are the servants of the Most High God who proclaim to you the way of salvation." Verse 18 says, "And this she did for many days. But Paul was annoyed, and turned and said to the spirit, 'I charge you in the name of Jesus Christ to come out of her.' And it came out that very hour." Yes, demonic possession can be a reality. Jesus dealt with it frequently in His ministry on earth. In our day, we are seeing a drastic increase not only in occult practices but in blatant Satanism.

Excommunication

Is it ever scriptural to excommunicate or disfellowship a person? 1 Corinthians authorizes excommunication for gross immorality and incest. Paul says, "Let him who has done this be removed from among you" (5:1-2), then he adds, "God judges those outside. 'Drive out the wicked person from among you'" (5:13). The Old Testament authorizes excommunication for improper sacrifices (Leviticus 17:3-4). Believe it or not, even declaring anathemas (curses) for false doctrines has a scriptural basis. Paul did it in Galatians 1:8–9. Fortunately, the use of excommunication is extremely rare in the Church today.

Images and Symbols

The question of why we have statues of angels and saints is sort of like asking why we have statues of George Washington and Abraham Lincoln. The saints are faith heroes. The statues are just reminders, not objects of worship. Exodus 25:17-22 speaks of images of the cherubim. In Numbers 21:8–9, Moses was told to make a bronze serpent and set it on a pole so that everyone who looked at the image would be healed of snakebite. (This image, by the way, became the symbol of the medical profession.) Just as Moses lifted up the bronze serpent in the desert, Jesus was lifted up on a cross, and we look to him for eternal life (John 3:14-15).

The Church I attended in St. Clair Shores, Michigan, was blessed for a time to have Fr. Bohdan Kosicki, a gifted artist, as pastor. He carved beautiful statues and symbols out of wood. They contributed greatly to the aesthetic and inspirational atmosphere of our church. Fr. Kosicki also used drawings, models, puppets, and other objects in almost every sermon. These things made his sermons much more meaningful and effective.

One of the beautiful symbols in the Catholic Church is the Pascal candle. Every year at the Easter Vigil Mass, the new Pascal candle for the year is carved and lighted in a special ceremony. The priest carves a cross in the candle with a stylus (or knife), between the points where grains of incense will be inserted. He then carves the Greek letter Alpha above the cross and the Greek letter Omega below the cross, and, between the arms of the cross, the four numerals of the current year (i.e., 2010). While carving these symbols, he says,

1. "Christ yesterday and today" while carving the vertical beam,
2. "The beginning and the end," while carving the transverse beam,
3. "The Alpha," while carving the letter A above the vertical beam,)
4. "And the Omega," while carving the letter Omega below the vertical beam.")
5. "To Him belongs time," as he carves the first numeral of the current year in the upper left-hand angle of the cross,)
6. "And the ages," as he carves the second numeral of the current year in the upper right-hand angle of the cross,)

7. "To him be glory and empire," as he carves the third numeral of the current year in the lower left-hand angle of the cross,)

8. Throughout all the ages of eternity. Amen," as he carves the fourth numeral of the current year in the lower right-hand angle of the cross.

9. The deacon then gives the grains of incense to the priest, who inserts the five grains into the places prepared for them, saying,
   A. "Through his holy wounds," (first grain);
   B. "Glorious," (second grain);
   C. "May he guard," (third grain);
   D. "And protect us," (fourth grain);
   E. "Christ the Lord. Amen," (fifth grain).

Priesthood

What about priestly celibacy and calling priests "Father"? It is true that Jesus said in Matthew 23:9, "And call no man your father on earth, for you have one Father, who is in heaven." He said the same thing about calling anyone Rabbi or Teacher in Matthew 23:8 and Master in Matthew 23:10. Jesus often used irony, exaggeration and shock to emphasize a point. Do you believe that if a person's eye causes them to sin, they should literally pluck it out? Do you believe that if their hand causes them to sin, they should cut it off? Of course not! Jesus said these things to illustrate the seriousness of sin. When he said do not call anyone your father on earth, he simply meant do not worship people or put them on a pedestal. Do not love your earthly father more than you love Jesus (Matthew 10:37).

The title "father" in the Bible was a title of respect for spiritual leaders. Jesus himself referred to Abraham as "Father Abraham" in the parable of the rich man and Lazarus (Luke 16:19-31). Paul calls himself the father of Onesimus in Philemon 10. In Acts 7:2, Stephen, the first martyr, refers to "brethren and fathers" and "Father Abraham." He refers to "our fathers" in Acts 7:11 and 7:19. Paul also addresses the people as "brethren and fathers" in Acts 22:1. In 1 Corinthians 4:15, Paul says, "For though you have countless guides in Christ you do not have many fathers. For I became your father in Christ Jesus through the gospel." In 1 Corinthians 4:17, Paul refers to Timothy as his beloved child in Christ.

The title "priest" in the early church is used in Acts 6:7: "a great many of the priests were obedient to the faith." Peter refers to a "holy priesthood" (1 Peter 2:5) and later to "a royal priesthood" (1 Peter 2:9).

As for the issue of priestly celibacy, this is one of the most difficult issues facing the Church today. In Matthew 19:12, Jesus says there are eunuchs who have made themselves eunuchs for the sake of the kingdom of heaven: "He who is able to receive this, let him receive it." Jesus called for a total commitment. He spoke of sacrifice, of giving up everything to become His disciple. That's what the celibacy rule is all about. Paul recommends celibacy in 1 Corinthians 7:25-38. He concludes with the words "So that he who marries his betrothed does well; and he who refrains from marriage will do better." Because Paul recommends celibacy for the sake of ministry, it is not surprising or unscriptural that the Church eventually decided that priests, being spiritual leaders, should remain celibate.

Whether we favor the celibacy rule or not, I think it is clear that when a man becomes a Roman Catholic priest, he has to make a serious sacrifice. He has to give up having a wife and a family. That is dying to self. It is not likely that a man will make that decision unless he has a deep, sincere faith and commitment to the Lord Jesus Christ and unless he is really sold out and living for eternity rather than for the fleeting pleasures of this life. It is a real witness and testimony of faith.

Being a priest does not make a man perfect. I will say, however, that some of the most remarkable, faith-filled, beautiful, sincere Christians I have ever met have been Catholic priests. They have a tough lifestyle to maintain in this hedonistic world. I certainly don't mean to demean marriage in any way. Married life and parenting obviously have their challenges too. But the rule of celibacy does make the Catholic priesthood a little more special and a little more like Paul's ideal— totally sold out to the ministry.

The Church has paid a great price for the celibacy rule. Right now, there is a severe shortage of priests. Many priests have left the priesthood because of the celibacy rule. It is probable that many others who might have become priests have chosen other vocations because of the celibacy rule. The Church certainly could change this rule without violating Scripture. Whether it will do so in the future remains to be seen, but to say the rule itself is unscriptural is untrue.

The idea of taking vows to the Lord also is not new. Acts 18:18 tells us that Paul cut his hair because he had taken a vow. Acts 21:23 tells of four men who were under a vow. In the Old Testament, there are several references to Nazarite vows (Numbers 6; Jeremiah 44:25). Although it is not required that we take vows, when we do so, God expects us to keep them. When we marry, we take a vow to take each other as husband and wife for better or worse, richer or poorer, in sickness and in health, in good times and in bad, until death do us part. God gives us the grace to keep those vows, and He expects us to keep them. Likewise, in holy orders, priests promise celibacy. In the religious orders, priests take vows of poverty, chastity, and obedience.

Women

Another area where the Church takes a heavy rap is with regard to the role of women. We certainly have seen some changes in this area since Vatican II. I expect that we will see more. In the pre-Vatican II era, women in the Catholic Church always wore a hat, scarf, or head covering of some kind in Church. This was in keeping with 1 Corinthians 11:4-15. Since Vatican II, this practice is no longer required. Actually, I don't think anyone ever officially changed the practice; women simply quit wearing hats to Church unless they felt like wearing them.

It should be noted that the same passage that speaks about women keeping their heads covered also speaks about women prophesying. Thus, it was recognized that there were women who had the gift of prophecy. There were also women deacons in the early church (Romans 16:1-2). Obviously, the Catholic Church has had women sisters (nuns) for a long time. Nuns minister in many different ways in the Church and have made tremendous contributions. Although I haven't actually taken a count, I would bet there are as many canonized women saints as men. Since Vatican II, we also have women serving as lectors and Eucharistic ministers. Actually, women serve the Church in just about every capacity other than as ordained priests and deacons. This also could change in the future.

Inflexibility

There is no question that the Catholic Church has a reputation of being inflexible on moral issues such as divorce, abortion, human rights, social justice, etc. Jesus was also inflexible on such issues. He was extremely strict on divorce (see Matthew 5:31-32; 19:3-9; Mark 10:2-12; Luke 16:18). In 1 Corinthians 7:10-11, Paul takes the same position that the Catholic Church has taken on the issue of divorce and remarriage: "To the married I give charge, not I but the Lord, that the wife should not separate from her husband (but if she does, let her remain single or else be reconciled to her husband)—and that the husband should not divorce his wife."

On the abortion issue, the Catholic position has consistently been pro-life. In fact, for quite a while, if you were anti-abortion, many people would assume you were Catholic. God is also strongly pro-life. When the murder of innocent children was officially sanctioned in the Old Testament, it was the final straw leading to God's judgment in the form of the Babylonian and Assyrian captivity of Israel and Judah (Psalms 106:37-42; Ezekiel 7:24; 9:9-10; 16:20-21, 35-38; 23:36-39, 46-49; 24:1-2). Aren't our unborn children the "least of our brothers and sisters" (Matthew 25:40)? If God is concerned when a sparrow falls to the ground, how do you think He feels about an aborted child (Matthew 10:29-31)?

The Catholic Church has a tradition of taking very strong positions on highly controversial human rights, civil rights, and social and economic justice issues. The point is, you don't change the rules to fit the desires of the people. Yes, it may be hard to live up to the ideals of the Gospel; in fact, it may be impossible. We all sin. We all fall short of the glory of God. We all need repentance, forgiveness, and salvation through our Lord and Savior, Jesus Christ. But sin is sin. It cannot be excused or overlooked. It must be confronted, admitted, confessed, and forgiven.

Conclusion

The Catholic faith is a deep faith. It is rich in symbolism and tradition. It is not always understood. It has not always been well explained. But to those who make the effort to understand the Catholic faith, it is beautiful and scriptural. We are a Church that remembers its roots in Old Testament Judaism. We are a Church of the past, the present and the future. If you combine the liturgy, the theology, the history, the symbolism, the music, the great faith heroes and the traditions of the Catholic Church with sound scriptural knowledge, and the power of the Holy Spirit, you have a very dynamic institution. As Paul says in Romans 11:33, "O the depth of the riches and wisdom and knowledge of God! How unsearchable are his judgments and how inscrutable his ways!" "Great indeed, we confess, is the mystery of our religion" (1 Timothy 3:16). God's word and ways boggle the mind. The deeper we go, the more we find.

"... sprinkle the water of expiation upon them." (Numbers 8:7)

CHAPTER VIII

Mary, Saints, and Angels

Can They Help Us?

Should we worship Mary, the angels, and the saints? Absolutely not! Catholic or not, we do not worship Mary, the saints, or the angels. We worship no one but God—Father, Son, and Holy Spirit. In Luke 4:8, Jesus says, "It is written, you shall worship the Lord your God and him only shall you serve." Exodus 20:2–3 says, "I am the Lord your God, who brought you out of the land of Egypt, out of the house of bondage. You shall have no other gods before me." Mary, the angels, and the saints are not mediators between God and us. Our only mediator is Jesus Christ. In John 14:6, Jesus says, "I am the way, and the truth, and the light; no one comes to the Father, but by me." 1 Timothy 2:5 says, "For there is one God, and there is one mediator between God and men, the man Christ Jesus."

What, then, is the role of Mary, the angels, and the saints? They are intercessors. The word "mediator" means intermediary or conciliator, one who brings about a settlement or conciliation. Jesus is the only one who could bring about conciliation between God and man. He bridged the gap between God and man by his death on Calvary. The word "intercessor," on the other hand, means someone who pleads or makes a request on behalf of another or intervenes on behalf of another. Is it wrong to ask Mary, the angels, and the saints to intercede for us? I don't think so. There is a big difference between worshiping a person and asking a person to pray and intercede for you.

The Bible encourages us to intercede and pray for each other. In 1 Timothy 2:1-4 Paul tells us,

First of all, then, I urge that supplications, prayers, intercessions, and thanksgivings be made for all men, for kings and all who are in high positions, that we may lead a quiet and peaceable life, godly and respectful in every way. This is good, and it is acceptable in the sight of God our Savior, who desires all men to be saved and to come to the knowledge of the truth.

Paul knew the importance of having intercessory prayer support for his ministry. In Romans 15:30-32, he says,

> I appeal to you, brethren, by our Lord Jesus Christ and by the love of the Spirit, to strive together with me in your prayers to God on my behalf, that I may be delivered from the unbelievers in Judea, and that my service for Jerusalem may be acceptable to the saints, so that by God's will I may come to you with joy and be refreshed in your company.

In Colossians 4:2-4, Paul says,

> Continue steadfastly in prayer, being watchful in it with thanksgiving; and pray for us also, that God may open to us a door for the word, to declare the mystery of Christ, on account of which I am in prison, that I may make it clear, as I ought to speak.

In 1 Thessalonians 5:25, Paul says simply, "Brethren, pray for us." In Philippians 1:19, he says, "Yes, and I shall rejoice. For I know that through your prayers and the help of the Spirit of Jesus Christ this will turn out for my deliverance."

The author of Hebrews also stresses the importance of intercessory prayer with these words: "Pray for us, for we are sure that we have a clear conscience, desiring to act honorably in all things. I urge you the more earnestly to do this in order that I may be restored to you the sooner" (13:18-19).

Paul himself was an intercessor. In Ephesians 3:14-19, he says,

> For this reason I bow my knees before the Father, from whom every family in heaven and on earth is named, that according to the riches of his glory he may grant you to be strengthened with might through his Spirit in the inner man, and that Christ may dwell in your hearts through faith; that you, being rooted and grounded in love, may have power to comprehend with all the saints what is the breadth and

length and height and depth, and to know the love of Christ which surpasses knowledge, that you may be filled with all the fullness of God.

Psalm 106:23 says that Moses "stood in the breach" to intercede for the people and to turn God's wrath away from destroying them.

Thus, we can all be intercessors for each other. We can pray directly to Jesus on our own behalf. We can pray to the Father in Jesus' name. We can pray "in the Spirit" (in tongues). And we can pray for each other. We can ask for our friends to pray for us. If we can ask our friends here on earth to pray for us, why shouldn't we ask our friends in heaven to pray and intercede for us? If you were applying for a job with a corporation and your uncle happened to be the president of that company, don't you think you would let him know you were applying and that if he could put in a good word for you, you would really appreciate it? Why shouldn't we do the same thing in our spiritual lives? We let our friends on earth know our needs and concerns so they can pray for us. Why shouldn't we do the same thing with friends in heaven?

Mary

The Bible doesn't say a great deal about Mary, the mother of our Lord, but what it does say is very good. Her soul magnifies the Lord (Luke 1:46). She has favor with God (Luke 1:28, 30). She is the handmaid of the Lord (Luke 1:38). God did great things for her (Luke 1:49). Jesus worked his first miracle at Mary's mere suggestion at the wedding in Cana (John 2:1-11). She didn't even have to ask. She just mentioned the fact that they were out of wine, and Jesus worked a miracle! Wouldn't you like Mary to suggest some of your needs to God? If you were out of money, sick, out of a job, or looking for a mate, wouldn't you like to have Mary mention that need or desire to our Lord?

I have a personal testimony in this regard. Back in my first year of college, before I had been born again, I was looking for a girlfriend and, eventually, for a spouse. I asked Mary to help me find the right girl. I gave her a complete, specific, detailed description of exactly what I was looking for, including religion, appearance, personality, sense of humor, even hair and eye color. At the same time, there was a girl named Kathy who was looking for a guy and she did the very same thing. She even specified that he should be an ex-seminarian. When I met Kathy, she fit my description to a T. She was (and is) the perfect girl for me. Kathy says I met all her specifications as well. I had even spent two years of high school in the seminary. What are the odds of that? We've now been married for over 40 wonderful years. I think Mary had a definite part in bringing us together. Ours truly is a marriage made in heaven. So if you're looking for a mate, instead of relying on the computer, why not ask Mary for some help?

Mary was present on Calvary when Jesus was crucified. Two of the statements Jesus made from the cross concerned Mary. John 19: 26-27 tells us that when Jesus saw His mother, and the disciple whom he loved standing near, he said to His mother, "Woman, behold your son!" Then he said to the disciple, "Behold, your mother!" And from that hour the disciple took her to his own home. Why did Jesus address Mary as "woman" rather than "mother"? I believe it was because Mary's role would be much broader from that time forward. She wouldn't just be regarded as the mother of Jesus (although that certainly would be awesome enough). She would be regarded as the model woman; a role model for all women of all time. Why was the disciple not identified? I think it's because the disciple represents all disciples of Jesus for all time. So Jesus is saying to us all, "Behold your mother." These statements of Jesus have been interpreted as an extension of Mary's motherhood to the entire Church. We should all invite her into our home, to look after us as a mother looks after her children; to intercede for us as a mother intercedes for her children. Mary was also in the upper room with the disciples in Jerusalem after the Resurrection as they devoted themselves in prayer with one accord (Acts 1:14). We can make Mary our prayer partner as well. Can you imagine a more powerful prayer warrior than Mary?

The virgin birth of Jesus is not only one of the greatest miracles in the Bible but a fulfillment of prophesies dating all the way back to the book of Genesis. In Genesis 3:15, God tells the serpent, "I will put enmity between you and the woman, and between your seed and her seed; he shall bruise your head, and you shall bruise his heel." This one short verse was the first prophecy of our Savior and his virgin birth. The Bible always speaks of "his seed" when referring to reproduction, not "her seed." Biologically, the seed is the male part of reproduction, the sperm which is planted in the egg and develops into a child. So in this one verse, where the Bible says "her seed," it indicates that our Savior would have no human father. It indicates that Mary's body would be specifically and miraculously prepared for virgin birth.

A more familiar prophecy of this miracle is Isaiah 7:14, which says, "Therefore the Lord himself will give you a sign. Behold, a young woman shall conceive and bear a son, and shall call his name Immanuel." The word for "young woman" in this passage is synonymous with virgin. The name Immanuel means "God with us," which of course is what Jesus was and is.

The Hail Mary prayer, our tribute to Mary, is taken almost entirely from the Bible. The term "hail" means to shout to in greeting or welcome; an exclamation of tribute; to greet with acclaim; a salutation. In other words, it is like a very enthusiastic greeting to a highly respected person. The angel's actual greeting in Luke 1:28 was, "Hail, O favored one, the Lord is with you!" Another word for unmerited favor is grace. Thus, when we say, "Hail Mary, full of grace, the Lord is with thee," we are in effect giving the same greeting as the angel. The next part of the Hail Mary, "Blessed art thou among women and blessed is the fruit of thy womb" is taken from Elizabeth's greeting in Luke 1:42. The remainder of the prayer is "Holy Mary, mother of God [Luke 1:43] pray for us sinners, now and at the hour of our death. Amen." When we say the "Hail Mary," we are not worshiping Mary. We are not asking her to save us. We are simply acknowledging her in the words of Elizabeth and the angel Gabriel, and asking her to intercede for us.

The Bible accounts of the wedding at Cana, the crucifixion and the upper room show us that Mary was very close to Jesus and that she is a powerful intercessor. When we pray the Hail Mary or the rosary, we are asking Mary to intercede for us as a mother prays for her child. How many testimonies have you heard of a mother's prayers for her children being answered? In the healing ministry, very often when a woman comes up to be prayed over, she is asking prayers not for herself, but for her children—for conversion, for a job, for healing, and so on. Those prayers are answered. That is a mother's love. My wife, Kathy, has a special gift of prayer. Her prayer life tends to be rather quiet and private, but very powerful. When she prays, she gets results. When we ask Mary to intercede for us, we are asking her to mention our needs as she mentioned the needs of the wedding hosts at Cana.

For many people, the rosary is a beautiful, Spirit-filled prayer. The full rosary consists of 150 Hail Marys, the same as the number of psalms. As the Hail Marys are said, the person meditates on what Jesus has done for us. The rosary is a perfect prayer for people on the go—in the car on the way to work, in a waiting room, etc. It is also a good public testimony against evils such as abortion, pornography, and social injustice. Some people don't even use the rosary beads. They just pray Hail Marys until they feel led to say an Our Father or Glory Be. Some people even alternate between Hail Marys and tongues as they contemplate the joyful, sorrowful, and glorious mysteries.

As an alternative, people may meditate on the Stations of the Cross or any aspect of Jesus' ministry. The rosary is also a way to pray together as a community. It has been associated with powerful movements of the Holy Spirit such as evangelization, conversion, healing, and peace. Even though we may not personally pray the rosary, who are we to criticize those who do if it aids them in their spiritual lives?

Has Mary actually appeared to people? I don't know. The Church is very cautious about stating that Mary has actually appeared. For example, despite considerable evidence, the Church has not yet officially pronounced that Mary appeared at Medjugorje. Interestingly, Medjugorje attracted considerable interest from Protestants as well as Catholics. As indicated previously, the Bible certainly contains many references to the appearances of angels and prophets. An angel appeared to Mary and Joseph. Jesus appeared to Paul. John, the writer of the Book of Revelation, saw many angels and saints in his vision.

Mary is the "handmaid of the Lord" (Luke 1:38). It is certainly possible that she could be used as a messenger of God. It seems unlikely that many people would "imagine" the same vision at the same time. If people say it is Mary who appeared to them, who are we to argue? We certainly can't disprove it.

In conclusion, Catholics don't worship Mary, but we revere her as a very special saint and a powerful intercessor who is especially close to Jesus. If other Christians want to ignore her, that is their business. But they should not condemn Catholics for acknowledging her and asking for her intercession.

Angels

When I was a child, I said the Angel of God prayer every night. It was one of my favorite prayers. The idea of this big, powerful angel assigned by God to protect me was very comforting. It was sort of like having an invisible bodyguard who was always with me. The prayer went like this: "Angel of God, my guardian dear, to whom His love commits me here, ever this day be at my side to light, to guard, to rule, to guide." But do angels really help us? What is our proper relationship to them? What does the Bible say about them?

Angels may be visible or invisible. In Numbers 22:22-35, the angel was invisible to Balaam but visible to his donkey. In Genesis 19, the story of Sodom and Gomorrah, the angels appeared in human form. Angels fight against Satan and his demons (Daniel 10:13, 20). They encourage us (Acts 10:3-5). Different churches have different angels assigned to them (Revelation 2:1, 8, 12, 18; 3:1, 7, 14). We are in their presence (1 Timothy 5:21).

What about guardian angels? In Matthew 18:10, Jesus says, "See that you do not despise one of these little ones; for I tell you that in heaven their angels always behold the face of my Father who is in heaven." So apparently children, at least, do have angels in heaven. What about adults? In Acts 12:6-11, an angel rescues Peter from prison. In Exodus 23:20-22, God tells Moses,

> Behold, I send you an angel before you, to guard you on the way and to bring you to the place which I have prepared. Give heed to him and harken to his voice, do not rebel against him, for he will not pardon your transgression; for my name is in him. But if you harken attentively to his voice and do all that I say, then I will be an enemy to your enemies and an adversary to your adversaries.

When Daniel was in the lions' den, God sent an angel to shut the lions' mouths, and they did not hurt him (Daniel 6:22). Psalm 34:7 tells us, "The angel of the Lord encamps around those who fear him, and delivers them," and Psalm 91:11–12 says, "For he will give his angels charge of you to guard you in all your ways. On their hands they will bear you up, lest you dash your foot against a stone."

Haven't you heard stories of people just narrowly missing a disaster and wondering how? Perhaps this has happened to you. I have heard of people hitting a patch of ice on a freeway, spinning completely around, going across three lanes of rush-hour traffic and not hitting anything. Could it be that there were angels nudging those cars around each other? Amy Grant has a great song about angels watching over us. Haven't you heard people testify of crisis situations when someone came out of nowhere and helped them out and then just vanished? Suddenly, the helper was gone and didn't even give their name. Could it be that

God has his angels patrolling the earth and helping Christians in distress? Why not? Hebrews 13:2 tells us, "Do not neglect to show hospitality to strangers, for thereby some have entertained angels unawares."

Angels intercede for us. Zechariah 1:12, for example, says, "Then the angel of the Lord said, 'O Lord of hosts, how long wilt thou have no mercy on Jerusalem and the cities of Judah, against which thou hast had indignation these 70 years?'"

Angels were active in the early church. In Acts 8:26, an angel tells Philip, "Rise and go toward the south to the road that goes down from Jerusalem to Gaza." The purpose of the trip was for Philip to meet an Ethiopian, witness to him, convert him, and baptize him. In Acts 10:3, an angel appears to Cornelius. In Acts 27:23-24 Paul says, "For this very night there stood by me an angel of the God to whom I belong and whom I worship, and he said, 'Do not be afraid, Paul; you must stand before Caesar; and lo, God has granted you all those who sail with you.'" The message of the angels is often to "fear not" and "take courage."

I believe angels are still active in the Church today. They are ministering spirits sent forth to serve, for the sake of those who are to obtain salvation (Hebrews 1:14). They encourage us, protect us, and intercede for us. Perhaps we are just too skeptical to recognize them.

The Saints

I know that in one sense of the word, all redeemed Christians are saints; but in this section, I am concerned with those individuals whom the Church has singled out for canonization, giving them the official designation of saint. They are our spiritual heroes, and we should acknowledge them just as we acknowledge our great national heroes. We have public holidays to honor people like George Washington, Abraham Lincoln, and Christopher Columbus. Likewise, in the Church we have feast days to honor the great saints. In the Bible, Hebrews 11 is sometimes called "The hall of fame of faith." It recites the faithful acts of several Old Testament faith heroes. We likewise should remember and celebrate the faithful acts and lives of Christian saints throughout the ages.

If you have never done so, I would encourage you to get a book on the lives of the saints. Their stories are very inspirational. They tell of great courage in standing up for their faith even under severe persecution, horrible torture, and death. They tell of lives of self-sacrifice, dedication, and prayer. The saints were people who were used by God as instruments of healing and miracles. They were very humble servants, models of virtue, great theologians, respected philosophers, etc. They were people who gave up everything the world has to offer—riches, pleasure, and material possessions—for lives of total commitment and service to Jesus Christ.

Throughout Church history, many holy people have been recognized with the title "saint." They show us what we could accomplish if we were willing to sell out totally and completely to Jesus. What was Mother Teresa but a simple, ordinary person who gave up everything to serve Jesus by serving the least of her brothers and sisters? So we honor the saints just as we honor our national heroes. But we don't worship the saints, just as we don't worship our national heroes.

Philemon 4 and 5 speak of having faith toward the Lord Jesus and toward all the saints. Hebrews 12:22-23, speaking of our spiritual status, says,

> But you have come to Mt. Zion and to the city of the living God, the heavenly Jerusalem, and to innumerable angels in festal gathering, and to the assembly of the first-born who are enrolled in heaven, and to a judge who is God of all, and to the spirits of just men made perfect.

The saints are the firstborn who are enrolled in heaven and the spirits of just men made perfect.

We know that the saints are alive with God in heaven. 1 Thessalonians 3:13 tells us that when Jesus returns, all His saints will come with him; thus, they must be alive with him now. In Matthew 22:30-32, Jesus says,

> For in the resurrection they neither marry nor are given in marriage, but are like angels in heaven. And as for the resurrection of the dead, have you not read what was said to you by God, 'I am the God of Abraham, and the God of Isaac, and the God of Jacob'? He is not God of the dead, but of the living.

In Philippians 1:21-23, Paul says that for him, to live is Christ and to die is gain. His desire is to depart and be with Christ. Thus, Paul recognized that to be absent from the body (physically dead) is to be alive with Christ in heaven.

The saints in heaven praise the Lord with the angels. Revelation 7:9–10 says,

> After this I looked, and behold, a great multitude which no man could number, from every nation, from all tribes and peoples and tongues, standing before the throne and before the Lamb, clothed in white robes, with palm branches in their hands, and crying out with a loud voice, "Salvation belongs to our God who sits upon the throne, and to the Lamb!"

Are the saints in heaven concerned about what happens here on earth? I believe they are very concerned. In Luke 15:7 and 10, Jesus says, "Just so, I tell you, there will be more joy in heaven over one sinner who repents than over ninety-nine righteous persons who need no repentance. . . . Just so, I tell you, there is joy before the angels of God over one sinner who repents." The saints and angels in heaven earnestly desire that every sinner repent and come to the Lord. Every time this happens, they rejoice and celebrate.

Do the saints in heaven pray for us? I believe so. I realize the Book of Revelation is a difficult book, but in it, John was shown visions of heaven. He tries to describe these dramatic visions to the best of his ability. In Revelation 8:4, he says, "And the smoke of the incense rose with the prayers of the saints from the hand of the angel before God." I don't know exactly what kind of communication system God has in heaven, but it seems that both the angels and saints are involved in it. Somehow, our prayers are received in heaven and are communicated to God directly and also indirectly through the saints and angels.

Saints do not work miracles by themselves. After a lame man was healed, Peter says in Acts,

> Men of Israel, why do you wonder at this, or why do you stare at us, as though by our own power or piety we had made him walk? The God of Abraham and of Isaac and of Jacob,

the God of our fathers, glorified his servant Jesus, whom you delivered up and denied in the presence of Pilate, when he had decided to release him. . . . And his name, by faith in his name, has made this man strong whom you see and know; and the faith which is through Jesus has given the man this perfect health in the presence of you all. (3:12-13, 16)

Again, we don't worship the saints, just as we don't worship Mary or the angels. Acts 10:25-26 says, "When Peter entered, Cornelius met him and fell down at his feet and worshiped him. But Peter lifted him up, saying, 'Stand up; I too am a man.'" In Acts 14:11-18, the people of Lystra came very close to worshiping Paul and Barnabas. They said, "The gods have come down to us in the likeness of men!" They called Barnabas Zeus; and Paul, because he was the chief speaker, they called Hermes. They wanted to offer animal sacrifices to Paul and Barnabas. When the apostles heard of it, they actually tore their garments and rushed out among the multitudes, saying, "Men, why are you doing this? We also are men, of like nature with you, and bring you good news, that you should turn from these vain things to a living God who made the heaven and the earth and the sea and all that is in them." They were scarcely able to restrain the people from offering sacrifice to them.

Conclusion

So Mary and the saints are alive in heaven with God and the angels. They are faith heroes. We revere and honor them, but we don't worship them. They are intercessors and helpers, not mediators. They are concerned about us. The angels are ministering spirits sent forth to serve God for our sake. They encourage us, they protect us, they inter-cede for us, and they serve as messengers.

Throughout the Bible, there are numerous examples of commu-nications between angels and humans. If we can communicate with angels, why can't we communicate with the saints? If some Christians (and some Catholic Christians for that matter) choose not to ask Mary and the saints to intercede for them, they don't have to. But they should not criticize those Catholics who choose to do so. We don't have to call on Mary or the saints for intercession, but this is an accepted tradition and it is scriptural.

CHAPTER IX

The Charismatic Renewal

Is This for Real?

I began this book with my personal testimony of being born again on January 29, 1976. There is another wonderful dimension to my testimony that occurred in 1983 when I was baptized in the Holy Spirit.

I doubted the gifts of the Spirit and resisted the baptism of the Holy Spirit for a long time after being born again. I didn't think it was necessary. I had asked to receive the gift of the Holy Spirit when I was born again. What more was needed? As for speaking in tongues and the other so-called gifts of the Holy Spirit, well that was okay for some, but not me. Again, my intellectual hang-ups got in the way. I didn't understand these Pentecostal, charismatic concepts; therefore, I wouldn't accept them.

Around 1983 I met a Christian attorney who was not only born again but was baptized in the Spirit as well. Here was this intelligent, dynamic attorney who spoke in tongues! It intrigued me. Bill was full of joy and love. His walk with the Lord seemed different than mine. Eventually, I joined his firm as an associate. He gave me some literature and tapes on the baptism in the Holy Spirit and the gifts of the Spirit. As I studied, all this "charismatic stuff" started to make sense.

One day Bill invited me to his church. It was a predominantly black Pentecostal church with a lot of hand clapping and foot stomping. The pastor was intelligent and articulate, yet entertaining and funny at times. His sermon was excellent, and I thoroughly enjoyed the service.

At the conclusion of the service, the pastor asked that every head be bowed and every eye be closed. He gave an invitation for anyone who had not been born again to raise their hand. I knew that didn't apply to me, so I kept my hand down. But then he said, "Some of you have been born again but haven't received the baptism of the Holy Spirit. I want you to raise your hands." I knew that did apply to me, so I raised my hand. Then he said, "I want all those people who raised their hands to come down to the front of the church. We're going to pray with you."

Well, you can imagine how conspicuous I would feel as a Caucasian walking down to the front of that black church and being prayed over. I quickly put my hand down. But, thanks be to God, I soon felt a gentle tap on the shoulder and opened my eyes to see a smiling usher motioning for me to come down.

I obeyed, and God honored that obedience. I think when we are willing to step out in faith, even though we feel foolish or conspicuous, God is gloried and His power is manifested. The pastor said a simple prayer over us. It wasn't anything spectacular. I didn't feel anything dramatic—yet. Then we were led into another room and people prayed over us in tongues. I soon found myself praying with them in tongues. When I came out of that room I felt like a different person.

That was my baptism in the Holy Spirit. Words simply can't do justice to it. It was an awesome, exciting, beautiful, mountaintop experience with the Lord. It changed my spiritual life. The gifts and fruit of the Holy Spirit began to be manifested in me. It wasn't anything I did; it was God. Since that time my life has been more joy filled (regardless of the circumstances) and more Spirit directed and controlled. I get more out of Scripture. It is as if God is speaking to me directly and personally every time I read His word. I have a greater love for people (even people I don't know and people who don't love me). Living as a Christian is more natural for me, rather than a constant struggle.

What Is It?

This Pentecostal experience of baptism of the Holy Spirit really isn't new. Origins of the charismatic renewal can be traced back to the turn of the century in a small farmhouse in Topeka, Kansas, where a small group of people were baptized in the Holy Spirit. In Los Angeles, a three-year-long revival began in 1906 at the Azusa Street Mission. Azusa Street ignited worldwide Pentecostalism. But the secular press really took note in 1960 when the Pentecostal experience broke out in middle-class Lutheran and Episcopal congregations. The movement also spread to the United Methodist church and the Presbyterian church in the United States.

Leaders of the Catholic Charismatic Renewal trace its beginning to Duquesne University in Pittsburgh, where a group of students met regularly with several professors to study Scripture and to pray. After two years of such meetings, the group, known as the CHI-RHO Society, agreed to make a retreat weekend together. It was on this retreat in February of 1967 that these people experienced the baptism in the Holy Spirit. They became the first Catholic charismatic prayer group. The gifts of the Spirit were poured out in them.

The movement quickly spread to Notre Dame, where home prayer meetings sprung up, encouraged and assisted by the Full Gospel Businessmen's Fellowship. Shortly after Easter in 1967, the First National Catholic Pentecostal Conference was held on the Notre Dame Campus. About 100 students, priests, and faculty members, chiefly from Notre Dame and Michigan State University, were in attendance. The gathering drew considerable publicity and became an annual event. Growth was phenomenal.

The Charismatic Renewal soon spread even more rapidly among Catholics than among the traditional Protestant denominations. The 100 of 1967 became 11,500 (including 7 bishops and 400 priests) at the sixth conference in June 1972. By 1973, the Charismatic Renewal Conference at Notre Dame brought some 20,000 enthusiasts to hear Cardinal Suenens, a Pentecostal himself, give a ringing endorsement of the movement. Catholic Pentecostalism had become a vigorous, international movement.

Many priests and nuns became involved in the Charismatic Movement. The movement spread throughout religious orders such as the Franciscans. Lives were turned around. Many anointed preachers and teachers were raised up. Characteristics of the movement included a new devotion to the Word of God, the traditions of the Church, and the sacraments. Charismatic worship is characterized by joy, enthusiasm, spontaneity, excitement, and love. Charismatics pray and sing out loud in tongues and in English. People are prayed over, and some are "slain in the Spirit" (so overcome by the power and presence of God that they fall down). From this movement of the Holy Spirit, healing ministries developed. Many books were written. A great deal of contemporary Christian music was produced. The Charismatic Renewal even developed its own magazine, *New Covenant*.

People involved in the Catholic Charismatic Renewal emphasize the necessity of personal commitment. You can't be a Christian by proxy—only by personal commitment. We must say "yes" to the baptism we received earlier in life. Strengths of the Catholic Charismatic

Renewal include a genuine conversion experience that leads to a living faith; a profound love of prayer; love of the Eucharist; and a renewed sense of discipleship. The Catholic Charismatic Renewal is a spark for transformation of the Church as a whole. People who receive the baptism of the Holy Spirit are very often called to various ministries in the Church such as teaching, lectoring, Eucharistic ministry, evangelism, prayer ministries, healing ministries, and other forms of service.

Is It Scriptural?

There are numerous references to the baptism of the Holy Spirit throughout Scripture. All four of the Gospels promise that Jesus will baptize believers with the Holy Spirit. In Matthew 3:11, John the Baptist says, "I baptize you with water for repentance, but he who is coming after me is mightier than I, whose sandals I am not worthy to carry; he will baptize you with the Holy Spirit and with fire" (See also Mark 1:8; Luke 3:16; John 1:33). In Mark 16:16-18, Jesus promises that various signs will accompany those who believe, including speaking in new tongues, casting out demons, and laying on hands for healing the sick.

Jesus himself was baptized in the Holy Spirit (Matthew 3:16; Mark 1:10; Luke 3:22; John 1:32; Acts 2:33). In fact, "Christ" means "anointed by the Spirit." In Luke 4:18-21, Jesus reads from the scroll of the Prophet Isaiah: "The Spirit of the Lord is upon me, because he has anointed me to preach good news to the poor" (Isaiah 61:1-2). He then announces that he is the fulfillment of this Scripture.

In Acts 2:3-4, we have the account of Pentecost, where the disciples received the promised baptism of the Holy Spirit: "And there appeared to them tongues as of fire, distributed and resting on each one of them. And they were all filled with the Holy Spirit and began to speak in other tongues, as the Spirit gave them utterance." This was the fulfillment of an Old Testament prophecy in Joel 2:28: "And it shall come to pass afterward, that I will pour out my spirit on all flesh; your sons and your daughters shall prophesy, your old men shall dream dreams, and your young men shall see visions." Note, it says that the Spirit will be poured out on all flesh, not just the early disciples. (See also Acts 2:16-18.)

Acts 4:31 tells of a prayer meeting where everyone present was filled with the Holy Spirit and spoke the Word of God with boldness.

In Acts 10:44-48, Peter is speaking to a group of people, and "the Holy Spirit fell on all who heard the word." "For they heard them speaking in tongues and extolling God." Peter recounts this to the apostles and brethren in Jerusalem in Acts 11:15-16. In Acts 19:1-7, Paul encounters a group of disciples who believed and had been baptized but had not yet received the Holy Spirit. Verse 6 says, "And when Paul had laid his hands upon them, the Holy Spirit came on them; and they spoke with tongues and prophesied."

Thus we see that baptism in the Holy Spirit is not only scriptural, but was the normal and expected course of events in the early Christian Church. Mary, Jesus' mother, was baptized in the Holy Spirit (Luke 1:35). She was present with the disciples in the upper room in Jerusalem after the Resurrection (Acts 1:14) and, by inference, was there when all the disciples were filled with the Holy Spirit on Pentecost (Acts 2:1). Elizabeth was also filled with the Holy Spirit (Luke 1:41).

There is a difference between "receiving" the Holy Spirit and "being baptized in the Holy Spirit." I once heard evangelist Pat Robertson describe it this way: "You can take a drink of water and 'receive' water, or you can dive into the ocean and be totally immersed in water." When we are born again, we receive the Holy Spirit, but when we receive the baptism in the Holy Spirit, we are totally immersed in Him. In John 20:22, Jesus breathes on the disciples and says, "Receive the Holy Spirit." Did they have the power of the Holy Spirit? Not yet. Did they speak in tongues? Not yet. John 20:19 tells us that the disciples were in fear before they received the baptism of the Holy Spirit. In Luke 24:49, Jesus tells the disciples to stay in the city until they are clothed with power from on high. In Acts 1:4-5, Jesus instructs the disciples not to depart from Jerusalem, but to wait for the promised baptism of the Holy Spirit. Later he tells them that they will receive power when the Holy Spirit has come upon them (1:8).

Thus, we see that the disciples "received" the Holy Spirit when Jesus appeared to them after the resurrection in John 20:22, but they were told to wait in Jerusalem until they received the baptism of the Holy Spirit. That did not occur until Pentecost (Acts 2:1-4). Acts 19:1-6 (cited above) is another illustration of the baptism of the Holy Spirit being separate and distinct from believing and being baptized.

Generally, the baptism of the Holy Spirit is administered through the laying on of hands. Acts 8:14-17 tells us:

Now when the apostles at Jerusalem heard that Samaria had received the word of God, they sent to them Peter and John, who came down and prayed for them that they might receive the Holy Spirit; for it had not yet fallen on any of them, but they had only been baptized in the name of the Lord Jesus. Then they laid their hands on them and they received the Holy Spirit.

Acts 8:18-20 goes on to say,

Now when Simon saw that the Spirit was given through the laying on of the apostles' hands, he offered them money, saying, "Give me also this power, that any one on whom I lay my hands may receive the Holy Spirit." But Peter said to him, "Your silver perish with you, because you thought you could obtain the gift of God with money!"

What About Those Spiritual Gifts?

First of all, what are the gifts of the Spirit? 1 Corinthians 12:7–11 lists the spiritual gifts of utterance of wisdom, utterance of knowledge, faith, healing, miracles, prophecy, discernment of spirits, tongues, and interpretation of tongues. Later, verses 27 through 31 list the additional ministry gifts of apostles, prophets, teachers, helpers, and administrators. Romans 12:6-8 adds service, exhortation, giving, and mercy. I don't think there is any limit to the number and variety of gifts the Holy Spirit can give us. 1 Corinthians 12:7 tells us "to each is given the manifestation of the Spirit for the common good."

One of the key teachings on the gifts of the Spirit is 1 Corinthians 14. Apparently (reading between the lines), the Corinthians overemphasized the gift of tongues, perhaps even above prophecy. It seems that they were quite proud of their spiritual gifts, as if it was something they accomplished on their own. Paul does not diminish the importance of the gift of tongues, but he explains its purpose and emphasizes how it should be manifested.

Today we sometimes hear that the gifts of the Holy Spirit were only intended for the early church, to "get it started." But we don't find that in Paul's writings or anywhere else in the Bible. To me, that position is illogical, inconsistent, and unscriptural. How can we say that every part of the New Testament applies to all generations except for this one part that only applied to the early church? It is true that our gifts are imperfect at this time and when Jesus returns and establishes his kingdom, these gifts will pass away because they will not be necessary anymore (1 Corinthians 13:8-10). But until that time, we need the gifts of the Spirit, and they should be welcomed and exercised in the Body of Christ. God didn't take the gifts of the Spirit away at the end of the apostolic age; we just became less open to the power, the presence, and the working of the Holy Spirit in our lives. The gifts of the Spirit are just as important for the Body of Christ today as they were in the early Church.

Healing

There are many Scriptures in the Old Testament and the New Testament dealing with the gift of healing. It is beyond the scope of this book to do an in-depth study of this gift, but it is worth mentioning that in Matthew 10:8, when Jesus sends his disciples out, one of the things he tells them to do is to heal the sick. In Mark 16:18, Jesus says that one of the signs to accompany believers is that they will lay their hands on the sick and they will recover. Thus, healing was definitely intended by Jesus to be one of the ministries in the Body of Christ. We know, of course, that a great deal of Jesus' own ministry involved healing the sick. In the Catholic Church, the sacrament of the sick is administered in accordance with James 5:14 by the laying on of hands and anointing with oil. In my former parish of St. Lucy, we had prayers for healing after Mass on a regular basis. We saw some dramatic results. As indicated previously, we also believe there is healing in the Eucharist based on 1 Corinthians 11:30.

Prophecy

With regard to the gift of prophecy, 1 Corinthians 14:1 says, "Make love your aim, and earnestly desire the spiritual gifts, especially that you may prophesy." Prophecy is definitely one of the gifts and ministries God has given to the church (Romans 12:6; Ephesians 4:11; 1 Corinthians 12:10, 28). The gift of prophecy was very prominent in the early Church, as seen throughout the Acts of the Apostles and the letters of Paul. We need this gift in the Church today as well. 1 Corinthians 14:3 tells us that he who prophesies speaks to men for their upbuilding and encouragement and consolation. This is a good test to use in discerning the prophecies we hear in the Church today. If the message is not upbuilding, encouraging, and consoling, it probably is not a true prophecy from God. While we should welcome and encourage the gift of prophecy, we should also test it and discern it.

Tongues

Probably the most controversial and misunderstood gift of the Holy Spirit is the gift of tongues. I believe this gift is controversial because it is a very powerful form of prayer. The enemy does not want us to use it. The gift of tongues is important because it releases and unlocks the power of the Holy Spirit in our lives. It is usually the first of the charismatic gifts received and manifested.

Romans 8:26-27 tells us that we don't really know how to pray as we ought. The Holy Spirit shows us how and what to pray. He intercedes for the saints according to the will of God. Therefore, when we pray in the Spirit, we are really praying according to the will of God. In my own experience, I have found that when I pray for someone in tongues, the Lord often gives me revelation as to how to pray for that person in English as to what they need, and so on. Sometimes we run out of words in English, or don't know what to say, or we are too tired or depressed or whatever to pray in English. Through tongues, we can still pray at those times and know that we are really pouring forth praise to God because the Holy Spirit is praying through us.

While manifestation of tongues is not essential to the baptism in the Holy Spirit, it is a sign or evidence that our community is receiving the outpouring of the Holy Spirit. When Peter visited Cornelius and heard the people speaking in tongues and glorifying God, he realized that they had received the Holy Spirit (Acts 10:46-47). Thus, Peter considered tongues as evidence of having received the Holy Spirit. So, if you speak in tongues, it is evidence that you have received the Holy Spirit, but if you do not speak in tongues, it does not necessarily mean you have not received the Holy Spirit.

In 1 Corinthians 14:5, Paul encourages us all to speak in tongues. When we speak in tongues, we speak not to men but to God (1 Corinthians 14:2). The gift of tongues edifies us (1 Corinthians 14:4). But in a service where nonbelievers are present, we should not all be speaking out loud in tongues, unless interpretations are given (1 Corinthians 14:23-25). At those times, we should pray quietly in tongues (1 Corinthians 14:28). When a message is given in tongues and then interpreted, it edifies the community. When that happens, it is a sign for unbelievers (1 Corinthians 14:22).

Paul tells us that he prayed in tongues (in the Spirit) and he prayed with understanding also. He sang in the Spirit and he sang with understanding also (1 Corinthians 14:14-15). He spoke in tongues even more than the Corinthians did (1 Corinthians 14:18). Ephesians 6:18 tells us to "pray at all times in the Spirit." Thus, tongues is a gift of the Holy Spirit and it is a great help to us. It is an important and powerful form of prayer and it should be properly used and exercised in the Body of Christ today.

Tongues is a prayer gift enabling us to pray at a deeper level. It is not, however, the only form of prayer. Charismatics also engage in liturgical prayer, Eucharistic celebrations, and other forms of public and private prayer and devotion. The gift of tongues should neither be given undue attention nor despised. The Catholic Charismatic Renewal does not insist that praying in tongues is necessary to the baptism in the Holy Spirit.

Fruit

We should never forget that as important as the gifts of the Spirit are, the best evidence of the Holy Spirit is the fruit of the Spirit. Galatians 5:22-23 tells us, "But the fruit of the Spirit is love, joy, peace, patience, kindness, goodness, faithfulness, gentleness, self-control; against such there is no law." If a person has really been baptized in the Holy Spirit, his or her life should be characterized by greater love, greater joy, peace in the midst of trials, more patience, more kindness, goodness, faithfulness, gentleness, and self-control. The common denominator of all spiritual gifts must be love. 1 Corinthians 13:1 warns us "If I speak in the tongues of men and of angels, but have not love, I am a noisy gong or a clanging cymbal." All spiritual gifts must be administered and manifested in love.

Summarizing the Gifts

What then should be our attitude toward the charismatic gifts? We sometimes hear people say, "If God wants me to have the gifts of the Spirit, I will have them." But God doesn't force his gifts on us. For example, God doesn't make us speak in English. Why should we expect him to make us speak in tongues? All of the gifts of the Spirit require some involvement on our part. Life in the Spirit is not passive. It requires active response to the prompting of the Holy Spirit.

1 Peter 4:10 says "As each has received a gift, employ it for one another, as good stewards of God's varied grace." 2 Timothy 1:6 tells us to rekindle the gift of God that is in us through the laying on of hands. In Ephesians 4:12, we read that the gifts of the Spirit were given "for the equipment of the saints for the work of ministry, for building up the body of Christ." Hebrews 2:4 tells us that the gifts of the Holy Spirit are a witness from God, and Ephesians 4:13 says we will need the gifts of the Spirit until we attain the unity of the faith and the knowledge of the Son of God and full maturity as Christians. That day has not yet come and probably will not come until Jesus returns.

1 Corinthians 2:14 says, "The unspiritual man does not receive the gifts of the Spirit of God, for they are folly to him, and he is not able to understand them because they are spiritually discerned." That is the attitude of the world toward the spiritual gifts, but it must not be the attitude of the Church. Paul tells us in 1 Corinthians 14:39-40, "So my brethren, earnestly desire to prophesy, and do not forbid speaking in tongues; but all things should be done decently and in order." 1 Thessalonians 5:19-22 tells us "Do not quench the Spirit, do not despise prophesying, but test everything; hold fast what is good, abstain from every form of evil." These Scripture verses are good advice for the Church today. Our attitude should be that we welcome the working of the Holy Spirit in the Church. We should not suppress the gifts of the Spirit, but we should discern them, test them, and hold fast to what is good.

Prayer Meetings

Throughout the psalms we see repeated exhortations to praise the Lord, to sing to Him, to sing a new song (not the same hymns over and over), to break into joyous song, to shout for joy, to clap our hands, to enter His presence with singing and dancing, to praise Him with various musical instruments, with clashing cymbals, to make a joyful noise, to give thanks to Him, to worship Him, to glorify Him, to proclaim His mighty works, to remember and tell of all He has done for us, to listen to Him, and so on. These are the very things we do in a charismatic prayer meeting. The psalms don't tell us to be quiet in church, to always be serious and reserved, to restrain our enthusiasm, to curb our emotions, or to avoid joy and excitement. I don't know of any place in the Bible where it says that church should be boring and painful. It should be joy filled, exciting, fulfilling, and uplifting.

Charismatic prayer meetings tend to have a general format. 1 Corinthians 14:26 says, "What then, brethren? When you come together, each one has a hymn, a lesson, a revelation, a tongue, or an interpretation. Let all things be done for edification." Ephesians 5:18-19 tells us to be filled with the Spirit, "addressing one another in psalms and hymns and spiritual songs, singing and making melody to the Lord with all your heart." 1 Timothy 2:8 says, "I desire then that in every place the men should pray, lifting holy hands without anger or quarreling." These are all characteristics of a charismatic prayer meeting. The Lord may give one person a particular hymn for us to sing. He may give another person a lesson or teaching to share. Others may receive prophecies or revelations for the group. Sometimes a prophecy will be given in tongues through one person and the interpretation will be given through another. Hands are raised in prayer and praise. The Lord may give some people Scripture readings to share.

There is a great deal of spontaneity in a charismatic prayer meeting, but there should also be a certain order along the following lines:

- Generally, we begin with praise, singing, and worship. The leader may share a particular Scripture or a particular theme that he or she feels led to give for that meeting.
- Next there is quiet time during which we wait upon the Lord for His Word to come forth in prophecy, Scripture, or revelation.
- Next comes a teaching.
- Following the teaching there is a time of sharing when everyone has an opportunity to share what the Lord has been doing in their lives.

- Following that, there may be a peace greeting.
- Then comes intercessory prayer and a closing song.
- Following the prayer meeting there is a time for fellowship and an opportunity for people to be prayed over for any particular needs.

The key is that everything should be done for the edification of the group and to give glory to God. We should never seek to draw attention to ourselves, but rather to glorify God.

Is It Catholic?

The Charismatic Renewal is definitely a part of mainstream Catholicism. It has received the blessing of several popes and the American bishops. A statement of the theological basis for the Catholic Charismatic Renewal was drawn up at an international conference in Rome. The statement notes that the Catholic Charismatic Renewal has as its basis the Gospel of Jesus Christ. The Holy Spirit and His gifts were accepted by the New Testament Church. The Church today preaches the same Gospel that was preached by the apostles. In our Creed we say we believe in one holy, catholic and apostolic church. We believe in the church founded by the apostles, which was literally a Pentecostal church. We should have the same awareness and expectation that the people had in the early New Testament Church. If we don't, we have lost something and we need to get it back. The purpose of the Charismatic Renewal is not to bring something new to the Church but to restore something we have repressed.

Pope Paul VI, speaking about the Charismatic Renewal, said that the Church and the world need, more than ever, for the miracle of Pentecost to continue in history. Nothing is more necessary in this increasingly secularized world than the witness of this spiritual renewal that we see the Holy Spirit evoking in the most diverse regions and milieus. He extolled the characteristics of the movement—intimate contact with God, commitment to prayer—particularly group prayer, shared prayer, praise, and thanksgiving. He cited the importance the apostle Paul placed on the spiritual gifts, and said,

> We are pleased to see signs of this renewal: a taste for prayer, contemplation, praising God, attentiveness to the grace of

the Holy Spirit, and more assiduous reading of the Sacred Scriptures. We are resolved and determined to open ourselves to the Holy Spirit to remove what is opposed to his actions, and to proclaim, in the Christian authenticity of our daily lives, that Jesus is Lord.

He translated a quote from St. Ambrose in the third or fourth century: "Joyfully we absorb, well-defined and well-moderated, the outpouring of the Spirit (*Laeti Bibamus Sobriam Profusionem Spiritus*)," concluding with these words: "Today either one lives one's faith with devotion, depth, energy, and joy, or that faith will die out.[6]

Conclusion

People today, especially young people, are looking for a church that is alive and real. If our worship is dead, they will leave; it is as simple as that. And who can blame them? We need the power, the gifts, and the fruit of the Holy Spirit. 2 Timothy 3:5 warns us of a time when people will hold the form of religion but deny its power. We need to guard against that. Our sacraments should be real community celebrations. Baptisms, confirmations, and marriages should not be private ceremonies; they should be celebrated by the entire parish. The sacrament of confirmation should see new power, responsibility, and gifts manifested in the confirmed. We need to see people converted in our church. We need to have a personal relationship with Jesus Christ. The churches that experience these things will grow. Those that don't will decline.

The Charismatic Renewal has helped to bring this power and spirit to the Catholic Church. It has been good for the Church, but it should not be a separate segment of the Church. The Charismatic Renewal should be absorbed by the Church as a whole. To a great extent, that has happened. We see it in our liturgies, hear it in the music, and witness it in the increase of Bible studies and other devotions and ministries in the Church. The year 2007 was the 40th anniversary of the birth of the Charismatic Renewal at Duquesne University. As we discussed earlier, 40 is a significant number in the biblical sense.

[6]Rev. Michael Scanlan, TOR, *A Portion of My Spirit.* MN: Carrilon Books, 1979, pp. 154-158.

The Israelites wandered for 40 years in the desert. The flood lasted 40 days. Jesus fasted 40 days in the desert. Forty years also signifies an entire generation in biblical terms; thus, we have had one complete generation in the Charismatic Renewal.

So where is the Charismatic Renewal headed in this generation? Perhaps a better question is, "Where is the Holy Spirit headed, and are we going to be open to it?" We have to let the Holy Spirit be the boss. Will there be another dramatic outpouring as there was in 1967? We don't know. Sometimes God is in the mighty wind and fire. Other times, He's in the still, small voice (1 Kings 19:11-13). As Jesus said, the wind blows where it wills, and so it is with the Spirit (John 3:8). We don't know where it comes from. It shows up unexpectedly. God works in many ways. We can't be like children in the marketplace, expecting God to dance to our tune (Matthew 11:16-17). We need to let God be God.

But we know that the early Church expected the gifts of the Holy Spirit to be manifested in believers. They recognized that these gifts were for the whole Church, not just a segment of it (1 Corinthians 12:28; Romans 12:6-8). I believe we should have the same expectation today. We speak of the gifts of the Holy Spirit in our services and sacraments, but do we really expect them to be manifested? Do we welcome them, accept them, and encourage them? When people are confirmed, do we expect them to receive gifts like tongues and prophecy? If not, why not? Do we pray over people for healing and really expect them to be healed? They may not always be healed instantly, but we should continue to pray and trust God for the healing. We need to cherish the Charismatic Renewal in the Church and embrace the gifts of the Holy Spirit. We need to teach our people about the Renewal and the gifts of the Spirit and encourage them to be open to them. I believe God wants those gifts for this generation and future generations just as much as He did for the last generation.

If I could wish one thing for every person who reads this book, it would be that everyone who has not already done so will receive Jesus Christ as their personal Lord and Savior and be baptized in the Holy Spirit. If you have not had these life-changing experiences, I hope and pray that you will. I urge you to find a Catholic Church in your area where you can take a Life in the Spirit seminar and receive these precious gifts. You will never regret it.

CHAPTER X

The Kingdom Divided

A Plea for Unity in the Body of Christ

Some time ago I was surprised by an invitation to appear on a Christian talk show to be interviewed as a "Spirit-filled Catholic attorney." After giving the matter some thought, I agreed. The program host, a Pentecostal pastor, said he didn't know what he was going to ask me. He would just pray and be led by the Spirit. I said that was fine; I would also pray and ask the Lord what He wanted me to say. I skipped lunch to pray and fast and get direction and guidance from the Lord. I followed my usual practice of writing a letter to God and writing down His response as I received it. Part of the dialogue went like this:

"Lord, is there anything specific you want me to say?"

"Tell them I love them. But I do not love their petty bickering, their quarreling. My desire is for people who will praise and worship Me from their heart, not just with their lips. There are those in My church who have knowledge of My Word but it hasn't sunk into their hearts. They argue about doctrine. They attack their fellow Christians. They do not speak out of love."

"Lord, is there anything else specifically about the Catholic Church?" (I expected Him to remind me about all the wonderful things that were happening in the Catholic Church at the time: the Charismatic Renewal, Marriage Encounter, Cursillo, Christian Family Movement, Vatican II, Scripture study, etc.). Instead, this is what I received:

"There is no Catholic Church in my eyes. There is only one church. My Body on earth. My church is a church of love. Where love is lacking it is not My church. My church is a church of joy. Where joy is lacking it is not My church. My church is a church of mercy. Where there is no mercy it is not My church. My church is a church of praise.

Where there is no praise it is not My church. My church is a church of My Word. Where My Word is not proclaimed, believed, and acted upon, it is not My church. It is man who has put labels on My church, calling it Catholic or Lutheran or Presbyterian or Baptist. Those are not My labels. It is man who has separated My body into pieces and fragments."

I am Roman Catholic. I love the Catholic Church. But I think one of the greatest sins and one of the greatest scandals in the Body of Christ is its lack of unity. Christians of different denominations attack each other, call each other names, and even accuse each other of being "unsaved" or "non-Christian." This grieves me, and I am sure it grieves the Holy Spirit. It definitely weakens our testimony to the world. It is amazing that we could totally disregard and violate a principle that is so dominant throughout the New Testament. Let's see what the Bible says about unity in the Body of Christ.

We're All One

The prophet Malachi in the Old Testament asks the following questions: "Have we not all one father? Has not one God created us? Why then are we faithless to one another, profaning the covenant of our fathers?" (Malachi 2:10). We Christians need to ask ourselves these same questions today.

1 Corinthians 12:12-13 says,

> For just as the body is one and has many members, and all the members of the body, though many, are one body, so it is with Christ. For by one Spirit we were all baptized into one body—Jews or Greeks, slaves or free—and all were made to drink of one Spirit.

In Galatians 3:28 we read, "There is neither Jew nor Greek, there is neither slave or free, there is neither male nor female; for you are all one in Christ Jesus." Romans 10:12-13 says, "For there is no distinction between Jew and Greek; the same Lord is Lord of all and bestows his riches upon all who call upon him. For, 'Everyone who calls on the name of the Lord will be saved.'" In Colossians 3:11 we see, "Here there cannot be Greek and Jew, circumcised and uncircumcised, barbarian, Scythian, slave, free man, but Christ is all, and in all." Perhaps we could paraphrase these verses, substituting "Catholic" and "Protestant" for "Jew" and "Greek."

Ephesians 4:4-6 tells us, "There is one body and one Spirit, just as you were called to the one hope that belongs to your call, one Lord, one faith, one baptism, one God and Father of us all, who is above all and through all and in all." In the Catholic Church, we sing a beautiful song based upon this Scripture. But do we really believe it? Do we practice it? 1 Timothy 4:10 says that Jesus is the Savior of all men, especially those who believe.

In 1 John, we see that every spirit that confesses that Jesus Christ has come in the flesh is of God (4:2) and that "whoever confesses that Jesus is the Son of God, God abides in him, and he in God" (4:15). It seems to me that that would include all Catholics and Protestants. Everyone who believes that Jesus is the Christ is a child of God (1 John 5:1). Doesn't that take in all Christians?

Causes of Disunity

Paul knew there would be dissension in the church. In Acts 20:29-30, he says, "I know that after my departure fierce wolves will come in among you, not sparing the flock; and from among your own selves will arise men speaking perverse things, to draw away the disciples after them." 1 Timothy 6:3-5 warns us about other causes of disunity:

> If anyone teaches otherwise and does not agree with the sound words of Our Lord Jesus Christ and the teaching which accords with godliness, he is puffed up with conceit, he knows nothing; he has a morbid craving for controversy and for disputes about words, which produce envy, dissension, slander, base suspicions, and wrangling among men who are depraved in mind and bereft of the truth, imagining that godliness is a means of gain.

Some people do seem to have a "morbid craving for controversy." They like to argue about words. There are those within the Body of Christ who like to focus on the minute points of disagreement between various denominations rather than on the points of agreement and unity. And, of course, there are those who preach godliness as a means of financial gain—the "God wants you rich" doctrine. Some preachers attack each other, envy each other, and regard each other as rivals. Philippians 1:15 warns about this: "Some indeed preach Christ from envy and rivalry, but others from good will." Jude 19 tells us that those who set up divisions are worldly people, devoid of the Spirit.

A second cause of disunity is simply having false information about each other. We haven't always communicated or explained why we believe what we believe. Another cause might be spiritual pride. We've always done things a certain way and interpreted the Scripture a certain way. We don't want to change. Change might be construed as an admission that we were wrong before. We don't like to admit that some other denomination just might have a better idea or a better interpretation of Scripture regarding a certain aspect of faith. I believe one of the greatest strengths in the Vatican II Catholic Church has been its willingness to change.

Jesus Emphasized Unity

In Jesus' great intercessory prayer for the Church in John 17, He prays for unity at least four times:

And now I am no more in the world, but they are in the world, and I am coming to thee. Holy Father, keep them in thy name, which thou hast given me, *that they may be one, even as we are one.* . . . I do not pray for these only, but also for those who believe in me through their word, *that they may all be one*; even as thou, Father, art in me, and I in thee, that they also may be in us, so that the world may believe that thou has sent me. (11, 20-21)

Later, in the same chapter, Jesus says,

The glory which thou hast given me I have given them, *that they may be one* even as we are one, I in them and thou in me, *that they may become perfectly one,* so that the world may know that thou hast sent me and hast loved them even as thou hast loved me. (22-23)

Only when Christians are one will the world stand in awe and see that Jesus is Lord.

In Mark 3:24-25, Jesus says, "If a kingdom is divided against itself, that kingdom cannot stand. And if a house is divided against itself, that house will not be able to stand." Satan knows this. If he can keep us Christians divided against each other, he can get us to destroy ourselves. In Matthew 11:16-17 Jesus says, "But to what shall I compare this generation? It is like children sitting in the market places and calling to their playmates, 'We piped to you, and you did not dance; we wailed, and you did not mourn.'" We want to fit Jesus into our mold. We want Him to "dance to our tune." We want a Baptist Jesus or a Pentecostal Jesus or a Presbyterian Jesus or a Catholic Jesus. But as Jesus told the woman at the well, the issue isn't where we worship but whether we worship in spirit and truth (John 4:21-24).

In Mark 9:38-40 John said to Jesus,

> "Teacher, we saw a man casting out demons in your name, and we forbade him, because he was not following us." But Jesus said, "Do not forbid him; for no one who does a mighty work in my name will be able to speak evil of me. For he that is not against us is for us."

If we're doing good works in Jesus' name, we're on the same side. Yes, we may differ in the way we do certain things, but as long as we're not against Jesus, we're for him. Fundamentalist Christians and Catholics are not enemies of each other. Our common enemy is Satan. Our enemy is atheism, not other Christian denominations. We should strive to convert the world to Christianity, not to convert fellow Christians to our denomination.

Paul Emphasized It

In 1 Corinthians 11:18, Paul chastises the Corinthians, saying, "For, in the first place, when you assemble as a church, I hear that there are divisions among you; and I partly believe it." In 1 Corinthians 1:10, he says, "I appeal to you, brethren, by the name of our Lord Jesus Christ, that all of you agree and that there be no dissensions among you, but that you be united in the same mind and the same judgment."

To the church at Galatia, Paul writes, "If we live by the Spirit, let us also walk by the Spirit. Let us have no self-conceit, no provoking of one another, no envy of one another" (5:25-26). Romans 14 deals with disagreements over rules pertaining to food. In verse 19, Paul sums up his dissertation in one sentence: "Let us then pursue what makes for peace and mutual upbuilding." Romans 12:9-10 says, "Let love be genuine; hate what is evil, hold fast to what is good; love one another with brotherly affection; outdo one another in showing honor." The command continues in verse 16: "Live in harmony with one another; do not be haughty, but associate with the lowly; never be conceited."

Philippians 2:2 says, "Complete my joy by being of the same mind, having the same love, being in full accord and of one mind," while 1 Thessalonians 5:11 tells us to encourage one another and build one another up. Paul concludes his second letter to the Corinthians with these words: "Finally, brethren, farewell. Mend your ways, heed my appeal, agree with one another, live in peace, and the God of love and peace will be with you" (13:11). We, too, need to mend our ways. We need to heed Paul's appeal to love one another, agree with one another, encourage one another, build one another up, and live in peace and harmony. We should strive for agreement rather than looking for points of disagreement.

Peter Emphasized It

There are only two books in the Bible specifically attributed to Peter (1 Peter and 2 Peter). Peter, however, addresses the subject of unity extensively in chapters 10 and 11 of Acts. The first great debate in the Church was whether Gentiles could join the Christian faith without being circumcised and following the Jewish traditions. In chapter 10, Peter has a dramatic vision that tells him that it is no longer necessary for the Gentile converts to follow the Jewish dietary laws and religious traditions. In Acts 10:34-35, Peter says, "Truly I perceive that God shows no partiality, but in every nation any one who fears him and does what is right is acceptable to him."

In Acts 11, Peter addresses the council at Jerusalem. He tells of his vision and explains how the Holy Spirit had fallen on the uncircumcised believers in Joppa. In verse 17, he says, "If then God gave the same gift to them as he gave to us when we believed in the Lord Jesus Christ, who was I that I could withstand God?" In 1 Peter 3:8, he concludes, "Finally, all of you, have unity of spirit, sympathy, love of the brethren, a tender heart and a humble mind." Who then are we to withstand God? We also must have unity of spirit and love of the brethren. As Christians, we all have the same Lord and the same Holy Spirit. We are all part of the Body of Christ.

It's a Sin

1 Corinthians 3:3-4 tells us that disunity is of the flesh. It says, "For you are still of the flesh. For while there is jealousy and strife among you, are you not of the flesh, and behaving like ordinary men? For when one says, 'I belong to Paul,' and another, 'I belong to Apollos,' are you not merely men?" 1 John 2:9 tells us, "He who says he is in the light and hates his brother is in the darkness still." Romans 2:1 says, "Therefore you have no excuse, O man, whoever you are, when you judge another; for in passing judgment upon him you condemn yourself, because you, the judge, are doing the very same things." We need to avoid disunity as a sin of the flesh. We need to remember that we all belong to Christ Jesus.

Warnings

The Bible repeatedly warns us to avoid dissensions and controversies within the Body of Christ. Titus 3:9 says, "But avoid stupid controversies, genealogies, dissensions, and quarrels over the law, for they are unprofitable and futile." Paul, in his second letter to Timothy, tells us to avoid disputing about words, which does no good, but only ruins the hearers (2:14), adding, "Have nothing to do with stupid, senseless controversies; you know that they breed quarrels" (2:23).

James 4:11 says, "Do not speak evil against one another, brethren. He that speaks evil against a brother or judges his brother, speaks evil against the law and judges the law. But if you judge the law, you are not a doer of the law but a judge." Romans 14:10 says, "Why do you pass judgment on your brother? Or you, why do you despise your brother? For we shall all stand before the judgment seat of God." Verse 13 of the same chapter says, "Then let us no more pass judgment on one another, but rather decide never to put a stumbling block or hindrance in the way of a brother."

Jesus gives this warning in John 16:2-4: "They will put you out of the synagogues; indeed, the hour is coming when whoever kills you will think he is offering service to God. And they will do this because they have not known the Father, nor me. But I have said these things to you, that when their hour comes you may remember that I told you of them." Persecution has come to the Christian faith. When the Antichrist comes, it will be even stronger. We need each other. We need to unite as the Body of Christ.

The Holy Spirit

Cardinal Suenens, a leader in the Catholic Charismatic Renewal, said that Ecumenism is the work of the Holy Spirit. One characteristic of the Charismatic Renewal is the strong thrust toward Christian unity. Within the Charismatic Renewal there are numerous ecumenical prayer groups, communities, and conferences. I believe that any church that is open to the Holy Spirit is going to have a burden for unity in the Body of Christ, because that is a priority with the Holy Spirit.

Back in July 1977, the Kansas City conference on Charismatic Renewal in the Christian churches brought together Baptists, Pentecostals, Presbyterians, Lutherans, Catholics, Episcopalians, Mennonites, Methodists, Orthodox Catholics, Messianic Jews, and nondenominational Christians. The bishop of the largest Holiness church in the world shared the pulpit with Cardinal Suenens, the cardinal archbishop of Malines—Brussels, Belgium.

Ruth Carter Stapleton, President Carter's sister, spoke before Francis MacNutt, a Dominican priest who was active in the healing ministry. Reverend James Forbes, a black Pentecostal preacher and professor at Union Theological Seminary, and Father Michael Scanlan, Franciscan priest and leader in the Catholic Charismatic Renewal and president of the College of Steubenville, also spoke.[7]

The Holy Spirit cuts through the denominational labels. Today we see the Catholic Church getting more and more into the Word of God.

[7]Rev. Michael Scanlan, TOR. *A Portion of My Spirit*, MN: Carrilon Books, 1979, p. 114.

At the same time, it seems that some of the Protestant churches are developing more reverence for the Eucharist, more involvement in the social gospel, more acceptance of the baptism of the Holy Spirit, and even more interest in the role of Mary and the saints. In the Catholic Church, we are seeing more emphasis on the concept of justification by faith and the importance of God's inspired Word in Scripture, more emphasis on the need for true repentance for sin and not just the sacramental action of absolution. The concepts of salvation, being born again, and baptism in the Holy Spirit are well developed in some Protestant denominations. Since Vatican II, these concepts have been developed more in the Catholic Church as well. We are also seeing a more balanced view of the role of Mary and the saints in the Catholic Church. Many of the obstacles that formed the basis for the Protestant Reformation have been removed.

Conclusion

The fact that there are four Gospels shows that although we all hear the same message, we hear it differently. We focus on different things. There is room in the Body of Christ for different traditions and different interpretations. They complement each other. We need each other. Catholics are wrong when they attack their evangelical and fundamentalist brothers and sisters. Fundamentalists are wrong when they attack Catholics.

Acts 4:32-35 tells us what happens when there is unity in the Body of Christ:

> Now the company of those who believed were of one heart and soul, and no one said that any of the things which he possessed was his own, but they had everything in common. And with great power the Apostles gave their testimony to the resurrection of the Lord Jesus, and great grace was upon them all. There was not a needy person among them, for as many as were possessors of lands or houses sold them, and brought the proceeds of what was sold and laid it at the apostles' feet; and distribution was made to each as any had need.

We may never reach this ideal again before Jesus returns, but we need to strive for it. Unity in the Body of Christ promotes power in the Body of Christ. Unity in the Body of Christ enables us to meet the needs of the poor and the hungry of the world. Unity in the Body of Christ promotes world evangelism.

When I was in college at Michigan State, I belonged to a folk music club called the MSU Folklore Society. We adopted as our theme a song written by Chet Powers and made popular by folk rock singer Jessie Collin Young. The chorus went "Come on people, smile on your brother, everybody get together, let's love one another right now." It may not have been intended as a Christian song, but it does have a Christian message. We need to smile on our brothers and sisters in the Body of Christ. We need to get together and love one another right now.

Let me close this book with the beautiful blessing of Romans 15:5–6, "May the God of steadfastness and encouragement grant you to live in such harmony with one another, in accord with Christ Jesus, that together you may with one voice glorify the God and Father of Our Lord Jesus Christ."

Epilogue

If you are a person who has left the Catholic Church because you felt or were told that it wasn't scriptural, I urge you to reconsider. If you have a loved one who has left the Church, I recommend that you encourage them to read this book. If you are a person who has criticized, condemned, or attacked the Catholic Church, I encourage you to take another look. If you are a Catholic who has criticized, condemned, or attacked other denominations, I urge you also to take another look. We are all brothers and sisters in the Body of Christ.

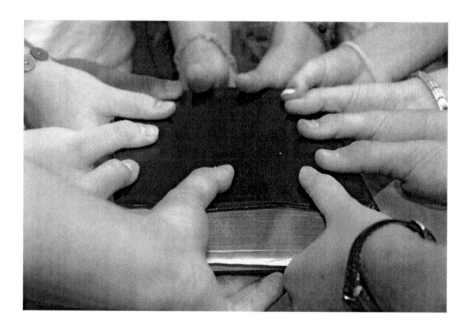

Bibliography

Benedictines of St. Andre d'Ottignies Brepols, 1981. American Editorial Commission Center for Pastoral Liturgy, The Catholic University of America. *The St. Andrew Bible Missal*. Brooklyn, NY: William J. Hirten Co., Inc., 1982.

Bokenkotter, Thomas. *A Concise History of the Catholic Church* (Revised Edition). New York: Doubleday, 1979.

Chilson, Richard. *An Introduction to the Faith of Catholics* (Revised Edition). Ramsey, NJ: Paulist Press, 1975.

Franciscan Communications. *The Catholic Church—Who Are We?* Los Angeles, CA: The Catholic Church Extension Society, 1986.

Hoever, Rev. Hugo H. S.O. Cist., PhD (ed). *St. Joseph Daily Missal*. New York: Catholic Book Publishing Co., 1959.

Lapple, Alfred. *The Catholic Church–A Brief History* (translated by Peter Heinegg). Mahwah, MJ: Paulist Press, 1982.

Redemptorist Pastoral Publication. *Handbook for Today's Catholic*. Liguori, MO: Liguori Publications, 1978.

Scanlan, Rev. Michael. TOR. *A Portion of My Spirit*. Minneapolis, MN: Carillon, 1979.

Shelley, Bruce L. *Church History in Plain Language*. Waco, TX: Word Books, 1982.

All Scripture quotations except those in Chapter IV are taken from the *Revised Standard Version of the Bible*. Camden, NJ: Thomas Nelson, Inc.

Scripture quotations in Chapter IV are taken from *The Deuterocanonical Books–Supplement To The Way.* Huntington, IN: Our Sunday Visitor, 1976.

"And it shall come to pass afterword, that I will pour out my spirit on all flesh." (Joel 2:28)

ORDER INFORMATION

LaVergne, TN USA
17 January 2011
212829LV00001B/26/P